.50

Why
Goats
Smell
Bad
and
Other Stories
from Benin

Why Goats Smell Bad

and Other Stories from Benin

Translated and
retold by
RAOUF MAMA

Illustrated by
Imna Arroyo

LINNET BOOKS
1998

Library of Congress Cataloging-in-Publication Data

Mama, Raouf, 1956–
    "Why goats smell bad" and other stories from Benin / translated
and retold by Raouf Mama ; with illustrations by Imna Arroyo.
        p.   cm.
    Summary: A collection of twenty folk stories from the Fon people
of Benin, about orphans and twins with magical associations,
spirits, animals, royalty, and farmers.
    ISBN 0-208-02469-7 (alk. paper)
    1. Fon (African people)—Folklore.   2. Tales—Benin.   [1. Fon
(African people)—Folklore.   2. Folklore—Benin.]   I. Arroyo, Imna,
ill.   II. Title.
PZ8.1.M2976Wh   1997
398.2′089′96337—dc21   97-30935
                                                              CIP
                                                              AC

The paper in this publication meets the minimum requirements
of American National Standard for Information Sciences—
Permanence of Paper for Printed Library Materials,
ANSI Z39.48—1984. ⊗

Designed by Abigail Johnston

Printed in the United States of America

To my mothers, the fairies of my dreams—
Rabiath Bachabi, Nourath Mama, Martine Hounsou,
Guezodje Beatrice, and Niara Sudarkasa.

And to Pascal Guezodje, Henry Penrose, Lester Ramsey,
Lyall Powers, Loretta Powers, and Dick Meisler—
friends of my youth.

Contents

Trickster Tales: Yogbo the Glutton

Preface

Why Goats Smell Bad and Other Stories from Benin is an attempt to recapture through the written word a sample of Fon tales from one of the richest oral traditions in Africa. It has grown out of my concern about the danger of permanent loss facing my country's oral tales, a concern which has led to a major project for the preservation of Beninese folktales. This book is the first offspring of that project.

Over a period of six years, I recorded numerous tales as told by Fon storytellers ranging in age from ten to sixty. As a native speaker of Fon and a professor of English with an M.A. and a Ph.D. in English language and literature, I have translated and retold the stories in this book from a unique vantage point that combines insights into the Fon oral tradition and familiarity with the conventions of English speech and composition.

Many non-Beninese readers may have heard of the kingdom of Dahomey and the Republic of Benin, but few are familiar with the culture of the Fon people or their oral tradition. It may be useful, therefore, to say a few words about certain particularities of these stories as well as the changes they underwent in their passage through the crucible of the translator's imagination.

Fon folktales have no titles. The titles of the stories in this book are my own, but in choosing each title I have ensured that it captures the essence of the story to which it is attached. Another important characteristic of Fon oral tales is that the storyteller, in opening them, likens them to a bird taking flight. The bird usually alights on the protagonist or the antagonist in the story. In an attempt to preserve that feature, I have opened many of the stories with "My story takes flight, over countries and kingdoms of long ago." That opening does not work with every story, however, and so I have used "Once upon a time," "Long ago," or some close variant whenever I felt that such a phrase would make the story flow better.

In translating into English the tales in this book, I tried to stay faithful to their cultural matrix and their moral. Only in a few cases, where I felt there was something to be gained in terms of clarity or narrative power, did I modify the stories in any way. These changes are explained in the notes that accompany each story. During the translation process I provided a great deal of description, however, with a view to conveying to non-Beninese readers and listeners some of the sights, sounds, and smells implicit in the stories.

In taking this liberty, I drew inspiration from Joseph Conrad, the great Polish novelist, who once wrote: "My task . . . is, by the power of the written word, to make you hear, to make you feel—it is before all to make you see. That—and no more, and it is everything." Conrad's powerful words capture for me the primordial obligation the storyteller must fulfill in venturing to set an oral tale down in writing.

This, then, is the background against which the stories in *Why Goats Smell Bad and Other Stories from Benin* should be read.

Acknowledgments

This book has been ten years in the making, and while I was gathering the stories and preparing them for publication, a great many people and a number of institutions gave me support and encouragement. Now that the book is finished, I want to acknowledge my debt of gratitude to them.

My thanks go forth to my mentor, Niara Sudarkasa, and to my teachers, both in Benin and in Michigan, for paving the way for this book, and to my colleague, Zossou Gaston, who gave me a helping hand at the beginning of my folktale project. I also wish to thank Professor Lyall Powers and his wife Loretta Powers for listening to my stories and making invaluable suggestions. Many of my colleagues at Eastern Connecticut State University also provided me with helpful suggestions. They are too numerous for me to name all of them, but I want to single out the following people for their generosity and their insights: Dr. Hugh Blumenfeld, Dr. Julie Nash, Dr. Barbara Molette, my friend Earna Luering, Mr. Ken Moorhead, Mrs. Leanna Loomer, Mrs. Kris Jacobi, and Dr. Sonia Marrero Cintron.

I am equally indebted to Professor Victor Kaplan, Mrs. Barbara Reed, to Mr. Bill Stuart, and to my students at Eastern Connecticut State University for being such good critics. I am deeply thankful to the University of Michigan for the grant that launched my folktale research project, to Eastern Connecticut State University and to the Connecticut State University system for their unflagging support and the numerous grants they gave me over the years. Thanks are also due to the National Endowment for the Humanities and the Connecticut Humanities Council for their grants. I want to take this opportunity to thank all those who attended my African Folktale Institute in summer 1996 for their vital contributions to my folktale research project. I would also like to acknowledge my debt to Professor David Philips; to Jill Oxendine, former editor of *Storytelling* magazine; to Richard Walker, storyteller and editor of *Facts and Fiction;* and to Bruce Frost, editor and proofreader.

I could not have completed this book without the support of my wife, Cherifath Mama, and our children, Faridath, Rabiath, and Gemilath. I want them to know how much I appreciate their love and understanding.

Although this book has taken ten years to complete, the groundwork for it was laid when I was a child listening to stories after the evening meal. That is why I want to extend special thanks to my parents, my relatives, and all the storytellers from my childhood, in whose company I wandered through the wonderworld of tales of long ago. Many thanks also go forth to Mr. Jean Pliya, from whom I have learned more than I can ever tell, and to my editor, Diantha Thorpe, for a job well done.

Finally, I wish to express my deep gratitude to Mrs. Martine Hounsou, Christophe Djotindagba, Thomas Tobossi, and to all the storytellers whose stories I have heard or recorded all these years. This book is a tribute to them and an attempt to capture through the written word in a foreign tongue the rugged splendor and the enduring power of the folktale tradition of our people.

Introduction

From the dawn of history, mankind has turned to folktales for relief from the toil and tribulations of daily life, as a means of preserving cultural tradition, and as a tool for instructing the young and preparing them for adult life. Folktales are the expression of people's vision of life and their sense of self. They tell the story of mankind's struggle in the ebb and flow of the human condition.

What James Baldwin, the noted black American writer, said about the blues in "Sonny's Blues," one of the greatest short stories ever written, applies to folktales as well: "They were not about anything very new. . . . For while the tale of how we suffer, and how we are delighted, how we may triumph is never new, it always must be heard. There isn't any other tale to tell. . . ."

Folktales are more than works of oral literature, however. They belong in the realm of cultural history as well, and therefore can serve as instruments for the promotion of cross-cultural understanding. In her introduction to *Favorite Folktales from Around the World*, Jane Yolen brings out the power of folktales for lowering some of the barriers that divide mankind against itself: "Folktales are powerful, they are a journey and a joining. In a tale we meet new places, new peoples, and new ideas. And they become our places, our peoples, our ideas." Julius Lester makes a similar point in his foreword to *Black Folktales*: "Folktales," he suggests, "are stories that give people a way of communicating with each other about each other."

Benin, a small West African country situated between Togo and Nigeria on the Gulf of Guinea, has a long and remarkably rich oral tradition that goes back countless centuries. The Beninese folktale tradition contains a wonderful world of places, peoples, and ideas, and it has a great deal to tell the world. But its ideas, its people, and its places have until recently remained unknown beyond Benin's borders to all but a few scholars. Benin's oral narratives have yet to be systematically recorded and brought into the mainstream of world oral literature.

Why Goats Smell Bad and Other Stories from Benin presents tales from the Fon, the largest ethnic group in Benin, who make up roughly three-fifths of the population. Other Beninese ethnic groups include the Yoruba, the Nagot, the Bariba, the Dendi, the Somba, and the Fulani. The Fon founded the kingdom of Dahomey in 1625, one of the historic kingdoms in West Africa. And because Dahomey was a major participant in the slave trade, Fon culture is shared to a greater or lesser extent by black people in the United States, Brazil, Cuba, Haiti, and other Caribbean countries.

The kingdom of Dahomey was colonized by France towards the end of the nineteenth century. In 1894, the French created the colony of Dahomey by joining the kingdom of Dahomey with a number of smaller kingdoms and colonial territories to the north and the south. Dahomey became independent in 1960, and like many African countries, went through a long period of political instability. In 1972, Mathieu Kerekou, a military commander, seized power and ruled the country until 1990.

In 1975 Dahomey was renamed the People's Republic of Benin, but when the military dictator was voted out of power in 1991, an event without precedent in modern African history, the country was renamed simply the Republic of Benin.

Many works have contributed to the preservation of Beninese folktales and paved the way for *Why Goats Smell Bad and Other Stories from Benin*. Among these, *Dahomean Narrative* (1958) by American anthropologists and folklorists Melville and Frances Herskovits, *Le Dilemme* (*The Dilemma*) (1983) by the Beninese scholar and folklorist Abdou Serpos Tidjani, and *La Fille Tetue* (*The Stubborn Girl*) (1982) by the Beninese historian, playwright, and short-story writer Jean Pliya, have been particularly helpful to me. These works and my own are important achievements in the struggle to save Beninese folktales from irretrievable loss, but much remains to be done. And the task is all the more pressing as the time-honored tradition of storytelling in Benin's households has all but gone out of existence. The colonial and post-colonial educational system, the stresses and strains of urbanization, increasing economic hardship, and the ascendancy of television have combined to bring about its demise. And with its passing, a valuable educational tool and an important source of entertainment have been lost.

Readers will recognize here echoes of well-known tales from the West and other parts of the world. "The Prince and the Orphan," for example, is strikingly similar to "Cinderella;" "When the River Becomes the 'Big Hole' " is an obvious variant of "Little Red Riding Hood"; and Yogbo, the protagonist in "Why Goats Smell Bad" and "How Yogbo Met His Death," calls to mind Anancy, Coyote, Fox, and other trickster figures. "The King Who Would Be God," the only one in this collection with distinct marks of the Judeo-Christian tradition, reminds one of "The Beggar King" in *Elijah's Violin* by Howard Schwartz, the prominent Jewish folklorist and poet. This folktale is in a class all its own, for it bears particular relevance to recent Beninese history and the rise and fall and the resurgence of General Kerekou, one of the most charismatic and fascinating African political leaders of our time.

"The King Who Would Be God" and a few other tales in this book are tales concerned with the spiritual side of life; some are fairy tales; others are cautionary or explanatory tales; and a handful are trickster tales. Whatever the motif, Beninese folktales always have a lesson to teach, and storytelling in Benin invariably involves debates during which listeners and tellers comment on the moral of the stories. In the Fon folktale tradition, virtue is always rewarded and vice punished. Fon folktales sound a warning against the perils of hatred, envy, greed, pride, egotism, sloth, and deceitfulness. On the other hand, they point out the rewards of love, compassion, self-sacrifice, courage, respect for the elderly, reverence for the sacred, discretion, and common sense.

In Fon folklore, human beings, beasts, plants, and spirits interact on a daily basis, and it is common for animals, trees, and spirits to take human forms to test, to punish, to hurt, or to help and reward human beings. Orphans, twins, and Yogbo the Glutton are common characters in Fon folktales. Orphans are usually abused by their stepmothers, but they enjoy supernatural protection and always conquer adversity. Twins are venerated as demi-gods. They are mysterious and unpredictable, and never given to idle chatter.

To the Fon, certain numbers—3, 7, and 41—have a special mythical function. In "The Dance of Poverty," for example, the spirit tests the protagonist three times, and in "The Name-Guessing Contest," Yogbo demands forty-one dishes as the price for telling his friend the names of the four princesses.

Yogbo is the archetypal trickster figure of Fon folklore. He is greedy, insatiable, mischievous, witty, and never to be trusted. He preys on children, and fools, and anyone who lets him, and the only way to get the better of him is through cunning.

Yogbo's gluttony and the troubles it gets him into point to the dangers of excessive love of food. Food is an important part of many Beninese folktales, not only because agriculture was and remains the main source of economic activity, but also because eating and drinking are central to the ceremonies marking the various events of life: births, marriages, deaths, reunions, and thankgivings. Food is for sharing, and those with food to spare have a duty to feed the hungry.

The stories in *Why Goats Smell Bad and Other Stories from Benin* are a valuable source of information about Fon culture and Fon customs and traditions. They shed light on the Fons' vision of life and the values they have lived by through the centuries. More importantly, however, these stories tell the timeless tale of how people the world over suffer, how they are delighted, and how they may triumph.

"Xo gé gé nyi xo a."

In the battle of words,
the man of few words wins the day.

—A Fon saying

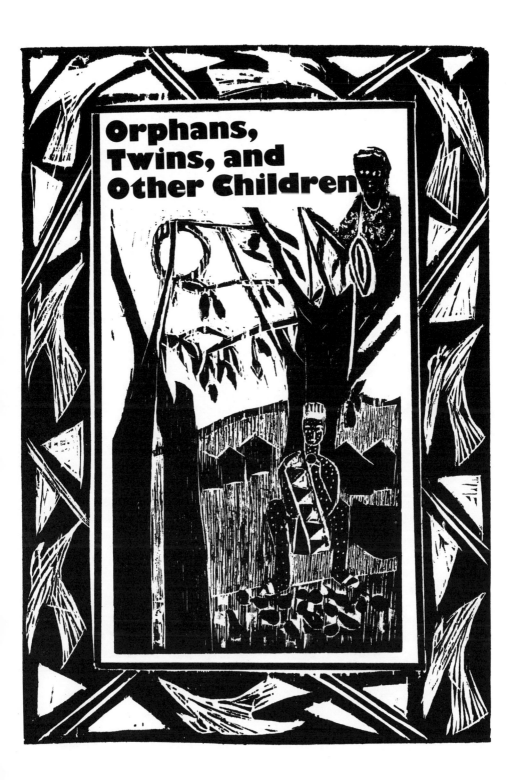

The Unwanted Child

My story takes flight over countries and kingdoms of long ago and alights on a prince named Hangnan-Hangnan-Gba, "Ugly-Bumbling-Pig." When he was born, the king found him so ugly that he would not touch him, not even with a stick! And the more Hangnan-Hangnan-Gba grew, the uglier the king found him, until he ordered his guards one day to abandon him in the jungle.

"Take him to the jungle and leave him there to fend for himself," the king thundered. "I cannot be father to such an ugly child!" He was a very powerful king, and he had forty-one wives and children without number. Throwing a child away was as easy for him as discarding an old piece of clothing.

No sooner had the king given the order than it was carried out, and Hangnan-Hangnan-Gba found himself, a mere child, among wild beasts in the heart of the jungle. All the animals were kind to him, and the ugly monkeys were so fond of the ugly boy that they adopted him. Feeding on wild fruits and roaming the jungle in the company of his new family, Hangnan-Hangnan-Gba grew up out of sight of all human beings.

A short distance from the jungle was another kingdom where a terrible drought had dried up the lakes and the rivers and scorched the earth. The drought went on and on, year after year, and there seemed to be no end in sight. Desperate for rain, the people took to sacrificing a beautiful maiden, once a year, to a huge serpent that dwelled in the jungle.

Decked out in beautiful clothes and priceless jewels, the sacrificial maiden would be accompanied to the edge of the jungle amid the singing of ceremonial songs and the beating of drums. Stepping bravely away from the followers, she would wave to them and plunge into the forest. Once she was lost to sight, the crowd would retrace its steps, and a few days later a little rain would bring a short break from the drought.

Hangnan-Hangnan-Gba was on the threshold of manhood the year the first maiden was offered as a sacrifice to the serpent. Hiding among the branches of the jungle canopy, he witnessed the horrifying ritual. Coiled around a baobab tree, the serpent unwound itself with stunning speed when the maid appeared and wrapped itself around her, crushing the life from her body. Hangnan Hangnan-Gba's blood boiled, and tremors coursed through him as the maiden's screams rent the air and the serpent hissed in triumph. "I must kill this monster," Hangnan-Hangnan-Gba muttered under his breath, his teeth clenched tight. "I must kill this monster and make the people free again."

For seven years, he learned to wield the bow and arrow with deadly, unerring aim. He taught himself to outrun the fastest beast in the jungle and perfected his skill in climbing up trees and swinging his way from one to another, quicker than any monkey. And while he was preparing for battle, he saw five more maidens sacrificed to the flesh-eating monster, one after another. Six times in a row, he tracked the serpent's movement from the heart of the jungle to the baobab tree where it waited for its victim.

The day the seventh victim was to be offered to the monster, Hangnan-Hangnan-Gba woke up at dawn, took his bow and arrows, and hid near the spot where the serpent used to lie in wait. Soon, it came writhing its way through the tall grass and the towering trees, its eyes blazing. Slowly, it coiled itself around its favorite baobab tree and waited. Quick as the wind, Hangnan-Hangnan-Gba let off a volley of arrows, piercing the monster's eyes and hitting it in the head and all over the body.

Hissing with rage and breathing fire, the serpent quickly uncoiled itself, thrashing about violently and crushing trees in blind pursuit of its enemy. But Hangnan-Hangnan-Gba had swung his way out of danger and taken cover in the top of a tree beyond the monster's reach. At last death overcame it, and it lay still. Hangnan-Hangnan-Gba cut off its tail, put it in a huge bag, and retraced his steps.

Shortly thereafter, the roll of drums, accompanied by ceremonial songs, was heard in the distance: a maid of unsurpassed beauty was being led to the jungle's edge as a sacrifice. But when she entered the forest, behold, the serpent was lying motionless in a pool of blood! And she ran back to alert her people.

The news of the serpent's death spread through the kingdom with magical speed, striking fear into the hearts of men, women, and children. "Who will provide rain to save my kingdom from hunger and thirst!" the king wailed. "Whoever killed the serpent has done a terrible thing indeed!"

By sunset, however, the sky had covered itself with blue clouds of the deepest dye, and soon water came tumbling down amid flashes of lightning and claps of thunder. When, after three days and three nights the rain finally ceased, the long drought was broken. The streams, which had long run dry, came back to life. And from one end of the kingdom to another, nature once again clothed herself in green. The king was now convinced that whoever had killed the serpent had saved his kingdom. Soon word went forth from the palace to the four corners of the region for the hero to come forward and receive his reward.

And so it was that Hangnan-Hangnan-Gba was proclaimed heir to the throne of that kingdom and offered the hand of the beautiful maiden whom he had saved from death. The king died shortly thereafter, and Hangnan-Hangnan-Gba was crowned king.

When Hangnan-Hangnan-Gba's father heard the news, he could not help taking pride in being father to such a hero, but the old king was also gripped by fear, for he knew he had done a terrible deed and that the day of reckoning was at hand. Years went by, and the king lived in dread of his son's retribution, but Hangnan-Hangnan-Gba showed no sign of any desire for revenge.

It came to pass, however, that the kingdom of Hangnan-Hangnan-Gba's father fell upon hard times and was attacked by a powerful rival to the east. The old king and his army fought fiercely and gave a good account of themselves, but the enemy was equally brave and would not be shaken off. Both sides sustained enormous losses. The battlefield was littered with rotting bodies, and an overpowering stench rose to the heavens. Myriads of vultures circled overhead, mingling their shrieks with the groans of those who lay dying and the cries of the injured. And still the two armies fought on.

In the end, the enemy's fighting spirit proved too much for Hangnan-Hangnan-Gba's father. His resources were depleted, his army was near exhaustion, and he found himself facing a hard choice: accept defeat or throw himself on the mercy of the son, Ugly-Bumbling-Pig, whom he had once cast out. "Better to die a thousand deaths than to lose my kingdom to the enemy," the king said. "Wounded pride may be mended within the family, but defeat at the hands of the enemy—that is the ultimate humiliation!"

And so it was that a messenger was dispatched to Hangnan-Hangnan-Gba's palace, bearing a desperate call for help:

"Hangnan-Hangnan-Gba, lend an ear, I pray,
To what I have to say.
Under the enemy's ceaseless rain of fire,
Your father's kingdom is rubble and mire
And may not survive another day!"

But Hangnan-Hangnan-Gba rejected his father's plea for assistance in a song he had been waiting to sing since the outbreak of the war:

"My father's favorite sons, where are they gone?
My father cast me in the jungle when I was born.
The beautiful ones, my father's beloved children,
Let them save the kingdom that has all but fallen."

No sooner had the first messenger left than another arrived, bearing an even more desperate call for help, for the war was going very badly for Hangnan-Hangnan-Gba's father. The enemy had massed his troops at the city's gates, and the kingdom was tottering on the brink of disaster. But the second messenger was received in the same manner as the one before him.

"My father's favorite sons, where are they gone?
My father cast me in the forest when I was born.
The beautiful ones, my father's beloved children,
Let them save the kingdom that has all but fallen!"

Still Hangnan-Hangnan-Gba's father, ever more desperate, persisted.

A third messenger was sent forth with a last, impassioned plea for help. The enemy had broken through the wall around the royal city, hand-to-hand fighting was raging in the streets, and the ancestral tombs were in grave danger of desecration.

The messenger's words at last stirred Hangnan-Hangnan-Gba into action. Marshalling his fearsome and highly disciplined army, he joined battle with his father's enemy. And so it was that at the eleventh hour, when ruin seemed but a hair's breadth away, the tide turned, the stranglehold on the royal city was broken, and the enemy was routed.

As Hangnan-Hangnan-Gba marched triumphantly into the royal city, people came out in their thousands to greet him. He was showered with praise and carried shoulder-high to the palace where his father was waiting. The old king's joy at the enemy's unexpected defeat was great indeed, but his remorse and sorrow over his cruelty to his son were greater still. With unsteady, faltering steps, the old man made his way toward his son and fell at his feet, weeping:

> "Hangnan-Hangnan-Gba, my son! My son, Hangnan-
> Hangnan-Gba!
> May God and the spirits of the dead bless you for saving
> The land of our forefathers from conquest and destruction!
> When you were a child, I found you ugly and threw you
> away!
> Your looks blinded me to the beauty within!
> May God forgive the crime I committed against my own
> child!"

There was much rejoicing that day and much weeping, too. A special ceremony was performed to celebrate the reunion of the king with the unwanted child and to make the son heir to his father's throne.

Hangnan-Hangnan-Gba, the outcast who became king and delivered his father from the clutches of the enemy, lived and died a long time ago, but his spirit lives on in the repeated telling of his story. Thanks to him, children are no longer thrown away, but valued as special gifts, no matter how unattractive they may at first appear.

There is an old Fon song *with this refrain: "There is no dumping ground for undesirable children. Whatever children are born to you are for you to keep." The Fon place a high premium on physical beauty, but they place an even higher premium on moral beauty. And no matter how ugly a child, he or she is valued as a human being. It is interesting that the child found so ugly by the king should be adopted by monkeys. This story is a cautionary tale, but it also expresses a belief enshrined in Fon folklore: that beasts are often more humane than people. Of course there are evil beasts, but there are more evil men and women. This story is the Fon variant of "The Boy Who Lived with Wolves," a Native American tale retold by Joseph Bruchac.*

The only significant change I have made is to the ending, where the unwanted child saves his father from defeat and there is reconciliation between them. In the original story, Hangnan-Hangnan-Gba ignores his father's plea for help and lets him go down to defeat at the hands of the enemy. I believe the change I have made gives the story greater power, for it allows for repentance and reconciliation without softening its condemnation of the king's initial cruelty to his son.

The Twin Princesses

My story takes flight over countries and kingdoms of long ago and alights on two princesses, Zinsa and Zinhoue, twin daughters of the king of Adja. They were very special twins, for one was born with a parrot's feather in her hair and the other had a silver bangle on her wrist.

One day, Zinsa cried out to her sister:

"Give me your bangle, or a lone twin will you be.
Our spirit companions are calling, calling to me.
'Come with us to the forest of bliss,' they say.
Only your beautiful bangle will make me say nay."

Twins were not given to idle chatter, and the girl's words struck fear into her parents' hearts. Zinhoue, too, was afraid. Never before had Zinsa spoken to her in that manner. She knew she must act quickly or lose her sister. So she replied:

"My beautiful silver bangle? That is not much to ask.
Though it is my birthmark, its removal is no task!"

But when she tried to take the bracelet off, it would not budge! She tried everything she could think of—water, oil, and soap; still, it would not come off. A superhuman silversmith had crafted it and put it where it lay, and only by superhuman means could it be taken away. Finally, when all attempts had failed, Zinhoue cut off her hand and gave Zinsa the bangle.

Zinsa did live, and years went by until the twins came of age. A more beautiful pair of maidens had never been born to a king, except that Zinhoue now had only one hand. One-handedness was a serious handicap to marriage in those days. No king was allowed to take a one-handed woman to wife. It was to Zinhoue, however, that a marriage proposal came, and by no less a personage than the king of Allada, their father's friend and ally!

When his friend asked him for his daughter in marriage, the king's astonishment knew no bounds. A king to marry a one-handed woman? Never in living memory was a king known to have done such a thing!

"You cannot marry my daughter," the king of Adja said, shaking his head. "A laughingstock will she be to your wives and the members of the royal family—and your marriage will be a breach of custom and tradition, a source of discord in your kingdom!"

To this the king of Allada replied, "Though taking your daughter to wife may fly in the face of tradition and arouse the wrath of a thousand venomous tongues, yet will I hold onto her and, through the power of love, prevail!"

The two kings argued for a long time. But the more objections the king of Adja raised, the more passionately the king of Allada pleaded, until at last the king of Adja gave his consent.

To be on the safe side, however, the king of Allada decided to keep the wedding a secret from all but a handful of his closest friends and advisers. Contrary to custom, even the king's other wives were kept in the dark. He knew that he would have to tell his council and his subjects that his youngest wife had only one hand, but such a thing was not lightly done. Until the time was right, he would have to keep the matter a secret.

So, the king was married in secret. His wives found it strange that none of them had been told about the king's wedding and that their youngest co-wife was introduced to them with both her hands hidden from view. But the strangest thing of all was the king's decision to have a special bathroom built in the palace, a chamber to which the newcomer alone would have access. That really set their curiosity ablaze and their tongues wagging. Some tried coaxing the king, some pretended to be Zinhoue's friends, and some took to eavesdropping, but nothing worked—the secret remained undiscovered.

Then, one moonless night, the king's eldest wife secretly made a little hole in the wall of the princess's special bathroom. And when the sound she had been listening for came—a faint, splashing sound of washing—she tiptoed over and peeped through the hole. And, like a thief who had snatched a long-coveted treasure, she stole away grinning.

She didn't have long to wait for an opportunity to expose the king and Zinhoue. The harvesting season was at hand, and a day would be appointed for the king's wives to take turns at pounding the king's millet for the royal storehouse. And so it was that the very day the king's crops were gathered in, his eldest wife, without consulting the king, fixed a day for the millet-pounding ceremony. She commanded messengers to spread the message to the ends of the kingdom.

The king of Allada was furious, but he had no choice but to go along with this decision. His secret had been found out, he was sure. How on earth was he going to weather the storm that was about to break over his head? The king thought and thought, but there seemed to be no way he could avert it.

Time went quickly by, and the millet-pounding festival was only a sunrise away. The king's eldest wife relished the moment to come when the people would find out that their king had married a woman who had only one hand! The king and Zinhoue, however, would have given anything to make time stand still and have the sun postpone his return across the wide sea.

Without telling her husband, Zinhoue resolved to take her fate into her own hand. So, at the midnight hour, when sleep held the king and the royal household in its grip, Zinhoue stole out of the palace and went forth into the forest, seeking death.

A short way down the path, she came upon a hungry panther, crouching low in the underbrush as it lay in wait for its prey.

"Kill me," the princess cried, "for life has become a burden to me." The beast asked her why she wanted to die and listened carefully to Zinhoue's tale of woe. Then he told her that he was unfit to touch a queen and urged her to go a little farther into the forest.

Trudging on, Zinhoue came upon a growling lion on the prowl. "Give me death!"she cried. "Life has become a heavy burden to me." The beast asked her why she was seeking death and listened carefully to her sad tale. Then, observing that she was a queen and that he had no power to take her life, he urged her to go a little farther into the forest.

Zinhoue moved on and soon came upon the guardian spirit of the forest, a huge fire-breathing serpent coiled around a baobab tree. "Strike me dead!" the young queen cried. "I will be better off dead than alive!"

"Why do you want to die?" the serpent hissed. So Zinhoue told him about her twin sister, how she came to lose her hand, her marriage to the king of Allada, and the plot to shame her publicly. "Give me death," she concluded. "I would rather die than be held up to ridicule!"

"Are you brave?" the serpent hissed, sending jets of flame blazing over Zinhoue's head. "Have you conquered fear?"

"Only shame do I fear," Zinhoue replied, shrinking a little from the serpent's fiery presence.

"Well then," the serpent roared, "the hour has come for you to prove it! If you pass the test, your eldest co-wife will be laid low, and all your enemies with her. And what is more, that which has brought you deep sorrow shall bring you joy in boundless measure."

So speaking, the serpent commanded Zinhoue to turn her back. Uncoiling himself, he circled around and ordered her to plunge first the stump of her arm and then the other hand into his yawning mouth. Swift as the wind, Zinhoue thrust her hand-less forearm into the fiery abyss, and when she brought it out, behold! Her arm was whole and encircled with golden bangles! She plunged her other hand in, and it too emerged equally adorned with golden bangles!

"Go home, and seek death no more," the serpent said, giving Zinhoue a golden pestle. "And when your enemies have all been laid low, you may return to give me an offering."

Stealing back to the royal bedchamber, Zinhoue carefully hid the jewelry and the pestle away. She wasn't going to say a word about the magical recovery of her missing hand. But the king had awakened from sleep and, having looked for her in vain, had started to worry.

"Where have you been?" the king asked.

"I slipped out for a breath of fresh air, my lord," Zinhoue answered, "for sleep had deserted me." At those words the king bowed his head, for he was a little ashamed for having slept while the hour drew near when the bitter cup of ridicule would be presented to them both.

As dawn broke over the royal city, there sounded a roll of drums, repeated at regular intervals, and accompanied by rustic songs of praise for the king and the royal family. Soon, the royal courtyard was crowded with men, women, and children wearing colorful garments. And when the roll of drums sounded for the forty-first time, the king, gaunt and sad-faced, went forth to preside over the age-old ritual of the millet-pounding festival.

Never had so many gathered together for these festivities. The king's eldest wife had done her work well. From far and near they came, in part to honor their king, but mainly to see with their own eyes whether this thing they had heard was true—that their king had married a woman whose right hand was missing!

When the signal was given, the king's wives, in order of seniority, took turns at pounding their share of the king's millet amidst much singing and dancing. They were all magnificently attired, but the most ravishing was Zinhoue. Rumor had enshrined in the minds of the king's subjects the image of a decrepit woman, but her shiny complexion, her graceful neck, and her beautiful, shimmering hair bespoke a flawless beauty.

There was a moment of uneasiness, an instinctive, collective holding of the breath when Zinhoue stepped forward. Then, swift as lightning, she cast aside the upper part of her attire, revealing a pair of shapely arms ablaze with golden bracelets and in her right hand a pestle superbly carved and glittering bright in the noonday sun. The crowd stood still, as if petrified, and in the hush that had descended upon the arena, she broke into song:

"The blackbird, who never rejoices at anyone's misfortune,
Who ever heard of the blackbird pounding millet?
Behold, the blackbirds have come to pound millet!
One flew from the north, one flew from the south,
One flew from the east, one flew from the west.
Who ever heard of blackbirds pounding millet?
Behold, the black birds have come to pound millet!"

Tongue-tied with astonishment, the king bounded up to his youngest wife. Then, as if crazed with joy, he rolled in the dust, begging her to pound him along with the millet. But Zinhoue was not for pounding the king.

The crowd surged forward, and clamors of astonishment and wonder rent the air. And so it was that the millet-pounding festival, contrary to what the king's eldest wife had intended, turned into a joyous celebration of marriage. And because the king had dared to marry Zinhoue when she had only one hand, his council decided that never again would a king be barred from marrying a woman for her physical features.

Amid the celebrations, the king's eldest wife was put under arrest to await trial. Zinhoue's father, the king of Adja, her mother, and all of their subjects rejoiced at the triumphant ending to her ordeal. But no one was happier than Zinsa her twin sister. Saved from death at the cost of Zinhoue's hand, Zinsa had lived to see her twin sister recover her hand and win enduring fame and glory.

In Fon culture, *twins are considered demi-gods. Whatever one does for one, one must do for the other. When a twin dies, he* *or she is said to have gone to the forest to fetch wood. It is taboo to weep or to say that a twin is dead. Twins are unpredictable creatures never given to idle talk. That is why Zinhoue does not flinch from cutting off her hand to give her sister the bangle she had demanded as the price for not returning to the spirit world. Zinhoue is a strong, compassionate woman who fears neither physical pain nor death. The only thing she fears is ridicule; she would rather die than be shamed. But this story is above all about self-sacrifice and the reward it brings to those who practice it.*

The Prince And the Orphan

My story takes flight over countries and kingdoms of long ago and alights on a prince. He was the king's only son, for all of the children before him had died, one after another. Two months before he was born, the king consulted the oracle according to custom, and this was what the royal diviner said:

> "A male child shall be born unto you.
> Let his name be a secret to him,
> To his mother, and to all your subjects.
> Only then shall he dwell
> In the world of the living.
> When he grows to manhood,
> A great many women shall yearn for his love,
> But only one has been ordained to claim it.
> She shall be his soulmate.
> Through their union alone
> Can he fulfill his destiny."

When the baby was born, the king held a secret naming ceremony with only his diviner in attendance, and the prince was named Denangan, which means "One of Them Shall Live."

Never was a more handsome prince born to a king, and he grew more handsome still as he drew near adulthood. He was tall and slender with a complexion like the blending of ebony and ivory. His voice was deep, his eyes keen and luminous, and there was a perpetual spring in his step. His smile, which disclosed a shapely row of dazzling white teeth, could touch a heart of stone with joy.

What made him the darling of the king's subjects, however, was his kindness and the unusual wisdom which shone through his words and deeds. He was an exceptionally gifted riddle-solver. In addition, he was known throughout his father's realm as a champion of the poor and the powerless.

When he grew to be a man and there came upon him a desire for a wife, the king let it be known that whoever could guess the prince's name would claim him for her husband. The glad tidings of the king's decision spread throughout the kingdom, touching with fire the imaginations of a thousand maidens.

Among these, there was an orphan named Hobami, "Woe Is Me"—the lowliest woman ever to fall in love with a prince. She was a tall, graceful girl with flowing, black hair, and big, brown eyes. Her stepmother, who had three daughters of her own, made Hobami work ceaselessly from the first light of dawn to the hour when witches, draping themselves in the colors of night, filled the air with blood-chilling cries.

Hobami's three stepsisters made no secret of their burning desire to marry the prince and had definite strategies for sweeping him off his feet. Their mother had ordered expensive clothes and jewelry so the sight of them would take the prince's breath away, and she planned to pay a diviner to reveal the prince's secret name.

As the contest drew near and their excitement reached fever-pitch, Hobami's stepsisters grew ever more boastful.

"From the moment the prince sets eyes on me, he will have eyes for no one else," said one.

"My smile will cast such a powerful spell on the prince that he will beg me to marry him on the spot," said another.

"When my turn to say the prince's name comes, my voice will sound so sweet in his ears that he will do anything to keep me by his side all the days of his life," the third sister said.

The voices of Hobami's stepsisters rang in her ears as she set off on one of her interminable errands, and she felt faint. Pressing her palms against her breast, she cried, "I wish I too had a mother who could find me a powerful diviner and dress me up as a princess! Then would my joy know no bounds, for I would not be my stepsisters' laughingstock, but their equal, worthy of the prince's love!" Hobami had no one to give her a helping hand, however, and she had to keep her own counsel.

On the day appointed by the king for the contest, Hobami's stepmother called her three daughters together and handed them the beautiful clothes and the priceless jewels she had bought especially for them. And while the three sisters were jumping up and down and screaming with joy, she called Hobami and gave her a bundle of rags, saying, "The king requires all the young women in the land to take part in the contest this evening. I would like you to dress up like everyone else, but this is all I could afford. You may go as soon as you complete your chores."

And while Hobami was busy drawing water, cleaning dishes, washing clothes, and sweeping the floor, her stepsisters washed themselves, rubbed their bodies with a fragrant ointment and lined their eyelids with antimony. Then, wearing their splendid garments and shimmering jewels, they called Hobami so she could see how beautiful they looked. "It's a pity we have to leave while you are still doing your chores . . . but we will put a palm branch at the crossroad so you will find your way to the palace without difficulty," they mocked. Then they set out for the king's palace and soon came to the crossroad. They knew that the path to the right led to the palace, but they put a palm branch across the path to the left and went on their way.

At a bend in the path, they came upon an old woman, a spirit in disguise. "My children, give me something to eat, for I am starving," she pleaded, holding out her withered hands in supplication.

"You witch!" one of the sisters snorted. "How dare you call me your daughter!"

"My mother is far younger and much more beautiful than you, old hag!" another sister hissed.

"You get out of our way before I pick you up and throw you into the bush!" the third sister roared. And the three sisters roughly pushed the old woman aside and moved on, hurling at her any obscenities they could lay tongue to and laughing at their own remarks.

The sun had vanished from the sky and darkness was slowly settling over the village when Hobami completed her final task. Quickly, she washed herself and put on the tattered clothes her stepmother had given her. The she wrapped a few bean cakes in banana leaves to still her hunger along the way and set out on the long journey to the king's palace.

She soon came to the crossroad her stepsisters had told her about and stood looking now to the left, now to the right, for the palm branch they said they would put across the path leading to the palace. Suddenly a whirlwind arose and enveloped

Hobami in an impenetrable cloud of dust. When it finally blew away, the palm branch lay across the path to the right. So Hobami turned right and went on her way.

She had hardly gone a few yards when she came upon the same old woman her stepsisters had insulted and ridiculed. The apparition stood across her path, her hands stretched out in supplication. "Give me something to eat, my child, for I am dying of hunger," she implored.

"I do not have much, but the little I have I'll share with you," Hobami replied. So speaking, she unwrapped the bean cakes she had brought with her and gave the old woman an equal share. "Now, if you will excuse me, I must be on my way, for I am late," Hobami said.

"Where are you going so late at night?" the woman asked.

"To the king's palace, to try my luck at guessing the handsome prince's name," Hobami replied. "But now that I think of it," she went on, "I haven't the foggiest idea what the prince's name is."

"I know the prince's name," the woman said, smiling gently and taking Hobami's hands in her own, "and since you have been so kind to me and given me food, I will tell you. Because all the king's children who were born before him had died in infancy, the king named the prince Denangan, which means 'One of Them Shall Live.' " Hobami thanked the woman over and over and begged her to say more about the prince, but she vanished, leaving Hobami dazed with curiosity.

When Hobami reached the royal palace, the last contestant was walking away, her head hanging in shame, to join the sorrowful multitude who had failed the name-guessing test. The sudden appearance of the ragged but comely girl drew sniggers and taunts from all round. Smarting from their own failure and exasperated by Hobami's daring in presuming to succeed where they had failed, the three stepsisters rushed forward and barred her way, their eyes blazing, their hair standing on end.

The king's diviner, who was in charge of the contest, sprang to his feet, ordered the sisters back to their seats, and, commanding the crowd to be still, motioned Hobami forward. "Do you know the name of the prince?" he asked her, smiling reassuringly.

"Denangan. That's his name," she stammered, her heart racing out of control. As she fell silent, there broke forth a roll of drums, and a thousand exclamations of wonder and amazement went soaring to the skies. The handsome prince came out from the secret chamber where he had been confined throughout the contest and walked toward Hobami, his arms open wide, his face bathed in a radiant smile.

Ashamed of their lack of kindness and fearful of Hobami's revenge, the three stepsisters and their mother fled from one village to another. But Hobami sought no revenge and left them to their own consciences. The cruelty of Hobami's stepfamily became the subject of numerous songs that followed the fugitives like a curse all the days of their lives. As for Hobami, she and her husband lived a long and happy life and had many children.

This is a close variant *of "Cinderella." In Fon culture, the person who takes responsibility for a child is called the stepmother, regardless of a tie of marriage, Orphans are said to have supernatural protection, provided by the deceased parent, and anyone who treats them badly will be punished. An interesting* *difference between the Fon variant of "Cinderella" and many of its counterparts is that Hobami was wearing nothing fancy when she arrived at the palace to take part in the contest. As in many stories in this book, names are very important. The name defines the person, and whoever knows your real name is believed to have power over you.*

The Orphan And the Leper

Once upon a time, in a village on the edge of the forest, there lived an orphan named Sehou. His father died before he was born, and he was a mere toddler when his mother, too, passed away. No hand ever soothed his brow when he was sick, no tender voice ever hushed his weeping, and no friendly smile ever cast its radiance upon him. Every day his stepmother made him do all the chores in the house and run countless errands. And never was he allowed to lie down until everyone else had gone to sleep and the night had come alive with the blood-chilling cries of birds of ill-omen.

One of his stepmother's favorite pastimes was to hand him a piece of black cloth and watch as he washed it over and over in a back-breaking, hand-blistering attempt to change its color from jet black to spotless white. Nothing gave her greater delight, however, than to watch from a distance as the orphan, gasping for breath and drenched in sweat, strained every muscle as he struggled hopelessly to fill a straw basket with water.

The stepmother's unkindness would have broken Sehou's spirit but for his dream of becoming a prosperous and well-respected member of his village community. And whenever that dream enclosed him in its magic circle, there was a spring in his step and a gleam of brightness in his eyes.

But as he grew older, the dream faded away, and sadness settled over Sehou. When he looked around him, he couldn't help noting how narrow was the path alloted to him by fate and how beautiful the wide road unfolding before everyone else. Each member of his age-group had a father to instruct him in the ways of the world, a mother to nurture him, brothers and sisters to share his joys and sorrows. Everyone had a female companion and a wide circle of friends to lend them strength when they needed strength and instill hope in hours of despair. But he had no one! He was all alone.

One day, Sehou's stepmother abused him so much that something gave way within him. And betaking himself to his room, he broke down and wept. Never before had the world appeared more bleak. "Better cast in my lot with the beasts of the field than dwell a moment longer in this village!" he cried. So he slipped out of the house and headed for the jungle.

As Sehou reached the outskirts of the village, doubt and fear overtook him. All of a sudden, it seemed to him that the trees, the shadows gliding on the green grass, and the birds flying across the clear, cloudless sky took to whispering among themselves:

"Behold, the fugitive orphan, the outcast
 In retreat from the world.
 Whither is he headed, the fool?
 To make his dwelling
 Among the beasts of the field, I suppose.
 What he could not find among his fellow beings,
 He is seeking in the wilds.

Where will he flee if the jungle casts him out too?
Where will he flee, the pariah, the fugitive orphan?"

Sehou stopped his ears and started running, but the faster he
ran the louder the whisperings sounded. A wave of self-pity
washed over him, and he felt an impulse to call upon Death to
take him away. Looking around, he saw in the distance a rope
dangling from a mango tree, and immediately decided to hang
himself. He climbed up the tree, tied one end of the rope firmly
to a branch, and made a noose at the other end. He was about
to slip his head through the noose when a growling in his stomach reminded him he had not eaten all day. So he reached out
and picked a handful of big, mouth-watering mangoes.

Once Sehou had eaten his fill, he dropped the remaining
mangoes and was slipping the noose around his neck, wondering how mangoes could be so tasty, when he caught sight of a
leper shuffling toward him. What a sad sight that leper made!
The disease had bitten deep into his toes and fingers, leaving
mere stumps. His skin was mottled with sores. His eyes, however, belied the triumph of disease over his emaciated body.
They were keen and bright and in constant motion, as though
the life that had once dwelled in his mutilated toes and fingers
had taken refuge there. A smile broke over his pock-marked
face as he caught sight of the mangoes the orphan had dropped,
and, skipping and bounding, he began a sing-song chant:

"I was hungry. Behold, God has brought me food.
 A moment ago I was contemplating death,
 But now I rejoice in being alive.
 Although leprosy has taken my toes and my fingers,
 I will hold on to life, for there is no knowing
 What bounties tomorrow may bring."

So chanting, the leper sat down under the tree and helped himself to mango after mango, eating with great relish. When his hunger was finally stilled, he put the few remaining mangoes in his bag and retraced his steps. Sehou, who had taken cover among the branches of the tree, watched as the leper walked away, stepping proud and whistling as though he were the happiest man in the world.

The leper vanished from sight as swiftly as he had come, but his behavior had left the orphan deep in thought. Sehou felt disgust and a dull ache of irritation. What did he mean, "You never know what bounties tomorrow may bring?" Tomorrow will bring nothing but more of the same, Sehou thought. That man allowed a handful of mangoes to delude him into false hopes of a brighter tomorrow! "If only I could catch up with him, I'd make him see the truth!" he cried.

He climbed down the tree and plunged into the woods. Hurrying through the bush like a man possessed, Sehou skipped over fallen tree trunks and holes, but the leper was nowhere to be seen. It was then that the notes of a rustic song caught Sehou's ear. Walking toward that song, he soon came to a field that stretched as far as the eye could see. The smell of rain was in the air, and a peasant family was hard at work planting. Gleaming black in the paling radiance of the setting sun, the soil had been shaped into furrows, pleasant to behold.

In the far corner of the field, the soil was still untilled. Bent double, and raising and lowering their hoes rhythmically, the peasant and his sons were plowing the ground into fresh mounds. Moving in line behind them, the peasant's wife and his daughters were burying seeds in the mounds, singing and chanting.

As the orphan stood and gazed at the scene, it slowly

dawned on him that he, too, could till a plot of land and, with God's help, become a respectable peasant, a good husband, and a responsible father. There was no knowing what bounties tomorrow might bring. He was so enchanted with the vision that he went right up to the peasant family and asked for a tract of land to till. They took him to the village chief, and his request was granted.

After several years of struggle and hard work, the orphan became a prosperous farmer, fell in love, and decided to get married. A wedding day was appointed, and the groom let it be known that it would be a day like no other. He hired a public crier and instructed him to travel the length and breadth of the kingdom, extending a special invitation to all lepers—a decision that set tongues wagging and heads shaking. His bride, his friends, his neighbors—everyone wanted to know why Sehou had decided to make lepers guests of honor at his wedding feast, but he evaded all their questions.

The wedding brought people from far and wide, for the bridegroom was exceedingly rich and the bride was from one of the most illustrious families in the land. What made it an event without parallel, however, was neither its splendor nor its luxury, but the huge number of lepers who had come. Never in living memory had so many lepers gathered together. At the height of the feast, when drink of all sorts was flowing freely and people were helping themselves to steaming, delicious dishes, and the whole arena echoed to the chatter and laughter of the feasting multitude, the public crier requested silence.

When stillness prevailed, Sehou stepped forward. Holding hands with both his bride and the leper, he told the crowd that this feast was not merely the celebration of a union, but also of a reunion. Then he explained how the leper had saved his life, and, turning to him, Sehou said, "Your childlike joy in living gave me a dogged will to live, trust in God, and hope for the future. And for these I offer you half my savings, half my lands, half my lifestock—an equal share of all that bears my name."

As the bridegroom fell silent, the crowd went wild with cheers, and a thousand exclamations of surprise, ecstasy, and wonder clashed back and forth. Astonished, his eyes bright with joy, the leper broke into a dance, skipping, leaping, and bounding. Then, imploring everyone to join him in prayer and celebration, he intoned:

> "I was hungry. Behold, God has brought me food.
> I was poor and God has brought me riches beyond
> measure.
> However fierce the wind of hardship may blow,
> Never let the flame of hope be snuffed out,
> For somehow, despair always returns to laughter.
> Give life a chance. Give life a thousand chances.
> There is no knowing what bounties tomorrow may bring."

This is an unusual variant *of the Cinderella story. The protagonist is a boy, however, and hope and perseverance do for him what the fairy does for Cinderella: They produce victory against the odds. An interesting feature of the story is the emphasis it lays on the importance of saying "thank you" to a benefactor. Gratitude is one of the virtues Beninese parents try to instill in their offspring. The orphan goes to extraordinary lengths in trying to express his gratitude to the leper who saved him from suicide and taught him the secret of success and hap-*

piness. Like the orphan, the leper is an outcast, and that is why the lesson he teaches the orphan is all the more powerful.

In traditional Fon society, lepers are a little like the "untouchables" in Hindu India. They are scorned and avoided. One of the most common misconceptions about them is that they can't keep secrets.

The Magic Drum

Once upon a time, an orphan named Sagbo lived with his stepmother and a stepbrother, Senan, in a village on the banks of a sacred river.

Sagbo was a good-natured, cheerful boy, even though he was not the favored child. Every day, his stepmother made him wash the dishes, gather firewood, and run countless errands, while Senan hardly lifted a finger.

"I like being useful," Sagbo always said. But Senan always bullied him and chanted as he worked,

> "A boy dressed in rags,
> His hair is wild grass,
> Have you seen Sagbo?
> His arms are teeny,
> His legs are skinny,
> Just like a mosquito."

Senan's tongue felt like a whip, but Sagbo would just shrug his shoulders and reply,

> "Tongues that love to bite and sting
> Cannot foretell what the future will bring.

Sooner or later, life will be better.
And my family's unkindness will not matter."

Then, one year it came to pass that a terrible drought struck Sagbo's village, burning its trees and its meadows, and turning its farmland to scorched earth. The village elders performed ceremony after ceremony, but not a drop of rain fell. Soon every barn was empty, and even the wild animals disappeared. The sacred river fell so low that only a few crabs and little fish were left alive.

Things got so bad, in fact, that the stepmother decided to save for Senan and herself what little food she could get. So she called Sagbo one morning and said,

"If you are hungry, find your own food.
Feeding you for years has done me no good.
Shelter I can provide, a place to rest your head,
But hunger and thirst are things you must dread."

That day, Sagbo slipped out of the house and went running to the shore of the sacred river where he hoped to catch a crab to still his hunger. But Sagbo found no crab. As he was retracing his steps, however, he stumbled upon three palm nuts gleaming black in the sun. "I'll eat these until I find something better," he said. But when he tried to crack one of the nuts with a stone, it flew into the river. So did the second, and the third one followed after it!

"Something strange is going on here," Sagbo cried. "I am going to find those palm nuts." The river was low and muddy, but he dove in and swam right to the bottom. There he saw an extraordinary sight: a village with green grass, leafy trees, and beautiful flowers. The sweet music of songbirds floated on the air. In the distance, the fish-scale roof of a mansion shimmered in the sun. Sagbo was amazed. "This is unbelievable," he said, feeling weak from hunger. "I am going to see who lives in that mansion and maybe he or she will share some food with me and my village."

And with these words, he made his way to the mansion, his eyes sparkling with wonder. At the gate, a plump, white-haired man inquired of Sagbo, "Where are you going, and what are you looking for?"

"My palm nuts fell into the river, and I am so hungry I want to get them back," he replied.

"Go in and tell the woman of the house about your palm nuts," the gatekeeper told him.

Sagbo went in and saw an old woman sitting on a stool sifting corn. Her hair was fluffy and white like cotton, and her face was wrinkled like a shrunken nut.

"Good morning, Nana," he said politely.

The old woman smiled a wide, toothless smile and said, "Good morning, child, what has brought you here?"

"My palm nuts have fallen into the river, and I want to get them back," Sagbo answered.

"I will help you find your palm nuts, but first you must pound some corn and prepare a meal for my household," she said, handing him a single grain of corn.

Sagbo stole a glance at the old woman. He knew that a meal could not be prepared from a single grain of corn, but he did not want to be rude. Carefully he put the corn into a mortar and pounded it with the pestle. Suddenly, his eyes grew very large, and his mouth fell wide open—the mortar had filled with all the flour he could possibly need! But he held his tongue.

With the flour and other ingredients the old woman gave

him, Sagbo cooked some food. But no sooner was the food ready than the cooking pot spoke to him.

"I want my share," it said.

Sagbo could not believe his ears. "Were you talking to me?" he asked, his heart pounding frantically.

"I want my share of the food," the cooking pot repeated. Then, suddenly, the dishes, and the bowls, and the water jar demanded the same. Soon, every thing in the old woman's kitchen was shouting at Sagbo for its share.

Sagbo was terrified and wanted to run away, but his skinny legs were too weak to go. He looked for a place to hide, but there was nowhere to hide. So, with shaking hands, he served food all around, and he was relieved to find the cooking pot and his companions very friendly. Then, he took the food that was left and shared it with the old woman.

After the meal, the old woman pointed to a room, saying, "Go into that room, child. You will find two drums—a big one and a small one. Take the small one. On your return home, beat it. It will bring you happiness."

Sagbo went into the room, took the small drum, thanked the old woman, and left.

When Sagbo came back ashore and beat his drum, steaming dishes suddenly appeared in front of him: pounded yam and fish stew, red corn-paste and roast chicken. Sagbo knew the magic drum could save the village. He did not stop to eat, but went straight to the palace to show it to the king.

In no time, the king's messenger was heard summoning the villagers to a feast in the royal courtyard. And for seven days, there was great rejoicing in the village and all over the kingdom. In gratitude for his gift to the village, Sagbo was adopted by the king, and numerous songs were made in praise of him. And the story of the adventurous boy, the three palm nuts, and the village at the bottom of the sacred river became famous throughout the land.

But not everyone was happy. Every song that was sung, every word that was spoken in praise of Sagbo, filled Sagbo's stepmother with envy. "My own son should have saved the kingdom and found favor with the king," she thought. So, she grabbed Senan and handed him three palm nuts, saying, "What Sagbo has done, you can do as well. Go to the bottom of the sacred river and bring back a magic drum. The bigger, the better."

And so it was that Senan cast three palm nuts into the sacred river, jumped in after them, and swam to the bottom. There, he found the underwater village and went running toward the mansion.

The gatekeeper asked him what he was looking for and told him to go to the old woman in the house. Senan went in, saw the old woman, and told her he wanted a magic drum like the one his stepbrother had brought to their village. The woman promised to give him a magic drum, too, if he would prepare a meal for her household.

But when she gave him a single grain of corn and told him to pound it into flour, Senan burst out laughing and said mockingly, "A single grain of corn to feed a whole household! This isn't enough to feed a baby chick!" So the old woman gave him a basketful of corn. But when the meal was ready and the cooking pot and everything in the kitchen started screaming for a share of the food, Senan went running to her. "What a stupid household you have!" he said. "Your cooking pot, your bowls, and your calabashes—everything wants a share of the meal!"

The old woman sighed wearily and went hobbling to the

kitchen, where she served everything in sight. Then she offered Senan the food that was left, but he wasn't interested in food.

"I don't want food," he said with a smirk. "I cooked the silly corn. Give me the magic drum so I can take it home right away."

So the old woman pointed to a room, saying, "Go into the room. You will find a small drum and a big drum. Take the small drum. On your return home, beat it and your wish will be fulfilled."

Senan ran into the room and grabbed the big drum instead. As he rushed out and headed for the gate, the old woman hardly had time to shout after him, "Should you run into trouble, say 'Bees and ropes, go back where you came from.'" Senan heard and wondered what the old woman was babbling about as he hurried home with his magic drum.

His mother was overjoyed when he came back home, carrying a big drum on his head. Beaming with pride, she helped him carry the magic drum to her hut and barred the door, saying, "Now, before the whole kingdom finds out about our drum and forgets about Sagbo's, let's fill all our pots and jars with food."

But it wasn't long before Senan and his mother were heard howling and screaming for help. And men, women, and children came running from all over the village. When the door was kicked down, a murmur of astonishment ran through the crowd; for a large drum stood in the center of the hut, and Senan and his mother were tied hand and foot with ropes, while a swarm of gigantic bees swirled around them, stinging them mercilessly.

The crowd looked on, helpless. Senan rolled about on the floor and screamed for a while before he finally remembered the old woman's parting words and shouted, "Bees and ropes, go back where you came from!" As soon as he did, the bees flew out of sight, the drum melted into thin air, and the ropes binding mother and son fell to the ground.

The stepmother became a laughingstock and blamed Senan for it. Senan, too, was ashamed and tried again and again to go back to the mansion at the bottom of the sacred river, but all he found were pebbles, and mud, and a few fish swimming to and fro. Of the mansion and the woman living there, he saw no further sign at all.

As for Sagbo, he grew up to be a member of the king's council and lived a long and prosperous life.

This story dramatizes the importance of kindness, respect for the elderly, and the need to keep one's tongue under control. Sagbo was kind-hearted, respectful, and could hold his tongue, whereas his stepbrother was unkind, rude, and unable to hold his tongue. More interesting in terms of the moral of the story, however, is the difference in outcome between Sagbo's and his stepbrother's journeys to the bottom of the magic river. Their motives are of great significance here. Sagbo was hungry, but so kind as to want to share his food with the whole village. His stepbrother, by contrast, was driven by envy and was greedy for fame and glory. The drum brings food on the one hand and bees and stings on the other hand. It as though the sound of the drum conveys a message from Sagbo and his stepbrother to the spirits who send the food, the bees, and the stings. In traditional Africa, drums were a powerful means of communication.

The Song Of the Spoiled Child

Once upon a time, there lived in the kingdom of Allada a widow and her grandson. The boy's name was Hingnon, which means "Slander Touches Me Not."

Hingnon was the son of the widow's only daughter, who had died in childbirth. And because she could not help thinking of her daughter whenever she looked upon the boy, she loved Hingnon more than anything in the world. Whatever Hingnon asked for, he was sure to get, for his grandmother denied him nothing, however whimsical or unreasonable the request. She had no will of her own whenever something caught Hingnon's fancy. She had no other wish but to please him.

One day, Hingnon saw the king's flock of sheep being led to the pasture. Plump and well-groomed, they moved gracefully across the landscape, their spotless fleece gleaming white in the sun. They were beautiful and pleasant to behold, but the most beautiful of all was the last of the flock, the one with a bell around its neck. As Hingnon stood and watched, his imagination filled with steaming dishes of roast mutton. His mouth watered, and he went running to his grandmother, crying, "Grandmother! Grandmother! Did you see that sheep? The big one with a bell around its neck? I want it slaughtered and roasted so I can eat it! Please, hurry, for I am very hungry! I am so hungry I can finish a whole elephant!" And Hingnon held his stomach, squirming and making faces as though countless crabs were clawing at him.

"Hingnon, your eyes are bigger than your stomach," the grandmother replied. "You cannot have the dish you crave unless I steal the king's sheep. And if I steal the king's sheep, you may never see me again, for theft is a serious crime. It is the law of the land. Let me go to the butcher's and buy some mutton which I will roast for you. Umh. . . . It will taste so good! Just wait and see," the grandmother concluded, smacking her lips and rising to her feet.

"No! I want the big sheep with a bell around its neck," Hingnon retorted, stamping his feet. "If you do not slaughter and roast the king's sheep for me, I will stop eating altogether. And then I will grow thin and die, and you will be responsible for my death." Because his grandmother did not run out in pursuit of the sheep with a bell around its neck, Hingnon started whimpering, and soon he took to screaming at the top of his lungs. And the veins in his neck bulged to breaking point.

The sight of Hingnon crying and screaming pained his grandmother unbearably. So she took her machete and set out in search of the sheep with a bell around its neck. She came back at nightfall, carrying the sheep on her back. Soon the mouth-watering smell of roast mutton, seasoned with pepper, onion, powdered shrimp and many other ingredients, filled their compound and spread through the neighborhood. Hingnon ate with great relish, cramming his mouth with chunks of delicious mutton and licking his fingers with loud, smacking sounds.

It was then that the voice of the king's messenger pierced the still night air: "The king's favorite sheep, the biggest and the most beautiful in the flock, the one bearing a bell around its neck, is missing. Let anyone who has seen it report its whereabouts to the king without delay. The king has sent his guards all over the city and to neighboring villages to search for it. Anyone who steals it or finds it and does not return it to the fold will endure the wrath of the king. A word to the wise is enough." And the message was repeated at regular intervals, sounding now faint, now loud, as the messenger moved from one section of the neighborhood to another.

Hingnon sat listening a moment, and then, he sprang to his feet and ran out of the compound in the direction of the messenger's voice, taunting:

"Sheep! Sheep! The king's favorite sheep!
I told Granny I must eat your meat.
Off she went in search of you.
She knew I would settle for nothing else.
She overwhelmed you by stealth,
And brought you home for me.
Your meat was delicious beyond words!
I ate and ate till I could eat no more.
Sheep! Sheep! The king's favorite sheep!"

Some of the villagers stood and listened in utter bewilderment, wondering what madness had come over the little brat. Others lingered a moment and then hurried out of earshot, as though the insolent words of Hingnon's song were more than human ears could bear.

Soon, reports of the song reached the king, and Hingnon was summoned to the palace. And there, in the presence of the king, his courtiers, and the members of the royal family, Hingnon repeated his song of ridicule:

"Sheep! Sheep! Beautiful sheep!
I told Granny I wanted you slaughtered
And roasted just for me!
I whimpered, and cried, and screamed,
And I would settle for nothing else.
Off she went, fast as the wind,
Quiet as a shadow.
And before you could say, 'Be-e-e-e-e,'
She had you strapped to her back,
And brought you home just for me.
Your meat was tasty beyond telling,
And your juicy bones— They were so delicious!
I ate and ate until my stomach bulged in ecstasy!
Sheep! Sheep! Beautiful sheep!"

The mouths of the courtiers dropped open. The members of the royal household gasped. The king was speechless. All were shocked by the daredevil insolence of Hingnon's song. When the king finally regained his tongue, he rose swiftly to his feet, his face a rigid mask of rage, and summoned his council to an emergency session. In no time the grandmother was arrested, tried, and sent to jail. Hingnon was put in the custody of the king and made to tend the royal flock from dawn to dusk—day in, day out.

So began a new life for Hingnon, the spoiled child. It was a life full of labor and toil—hard and strenuous, a far cry from the life of overindulgence he had once lived in his grandmother's lap.

This story is told to warn *parents and guardians against indulging a child. That the grandmother was sent to prison dramatizes the belief among the Fon that the adult who spoils a child is morally responsible for the child's behavior.*

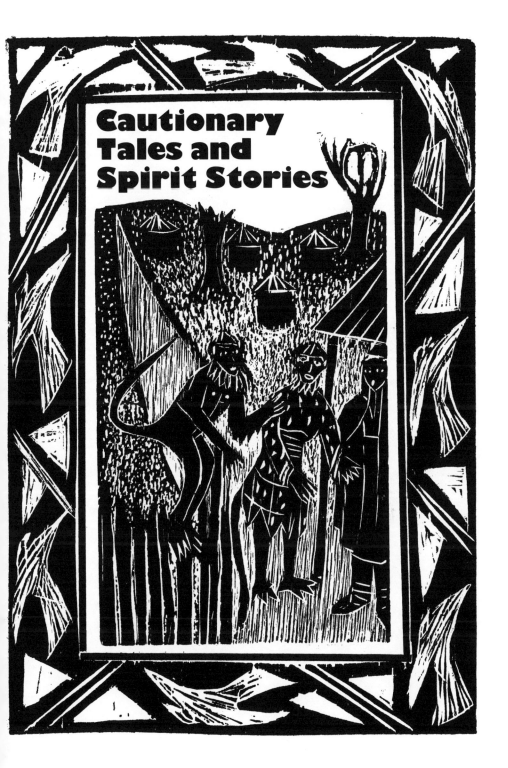

Cautionary Tales and Spirit Stories

The Dance Of Poverty

My story takes flight over countries and kingdoms of long ago and alights in a village where once there lived a poor peasant farmer named Atchanminanguey. Hunger made his stomach cling to his back. His clothes were ragged, his shoes were worn through, and he lived in a miserable shack all by himself on the outskirts of the village.

One hot, sunny day, as Atchanminanguey was returning from his cornfield, he felt faint and went staggering to a tree for support, crying, "I wish I could get rich one day! Then life would not be such a burden to me!"

No sooner had he spoken those words than an exceedingly tall, lanky man dressed in spotless white stood before him. His head was misshapen, his eyes were hollow, and his neck was very, very long. Atchanminanguey felt chills coursing down his back, and he wanted to run away, but his legs seemed to have turned to water.

"I mean no harm, Atchanminanguey," the spirit said reassuringly. "I heard your wish and I have come to make you happy." The spirit then handed Atchanminanguey seven little gourds and added, "Smash these to the ground one by one along the way, but the last one you must not throw to the ground until you reach the place where you wish to make your dwelling. I give you these without asking for anything in return, except that you sacrifice a pigeon and a duck for me every year of your life."

"I will sacrifice a pigeon and a duck for you not once, not twice, but three times a year, as long as I live," Atchaninman-guey said, trembling. Then he thanked the spirit and hurried on his way without daring to look back.

When he smashed the first gourd to the ground, Atchanmi-nanguey was transformed into a king wearing a crown of gold and garments of finest silk. To his right and to his left and behind him were guards and courtiers singing and showering him with praise. Atchanminanguey gazed all around at the spirit's wonderful gifts, and his head swelled with pride. After he had walked a short distance, he broke the second gourd and found himself in the company of men and women carrying trunks filled with diamonds, gold, silver, and priceless cloths.

The third gourd brought him lovely wives and beautiful children, and out of the fourth gourd there sprung a large herd of cattle guarded by herdsmen. When he broke the fifth one, Atchanminanguey became the owner of an orchard spreading as far as the eye could see. The sixth gourd brought him a vast farm teeming with sheep, goats, chickens, ducks, turkeys, guinea fowls, and pigeons. When finally he smashed the seventh gourd to the ground, a gorgeous palace stood where once his crumbling shack had been. Atchanminanguey surveyed all that the spirit had given him, and his joy knew no bounds.

Having risen in a few brief hours from great poverty to great wealth, Atchanminanguey lived happily for years, surrounded by his wives, his children, and his servants. His name was the subject of countless praise-songs, and every day crowds of friends, relatives, and well-wishers came streaming to his palace to pay their respects.

In the evening, to the spellbinding sound of royal drums, Atchanminanguey's magnificent courtyard would turn into a dance floor, where the rich and powerful competed against each other for the best dancer's trophy. Many a talented dancer put on a dazzling display of graceful, majestic steps, but Atchanminanguey invariably claimed the prize, for he was the best dancer of all. His wish to become rich had been fulfilled, but he had forgotten his promise of sacrifice to the spirit to whom he owed his good fortune.

One day, a man dressed in rags came to the palace as Atchanminanguey was sitting down to lunch and asked him for a pigeon and a duck. Atchanminanguey looked at the dishevelled stranger with contempt and scolded him:

> "I am not a merchant of ducks and pigeons,
> Nor am I giving any away!
> You have come to the wrong place!
> And your presence in my palace is a disgrace!"

And the stranger was driven from the palace empty-handed.

A year later, another stranger wearing tattered clothes came to the palace as Atchanminanguey was about to have lunch and asked for a pigeon and a duck. But Atchanminanguey was no more inclined to generosity than he had been a year before, and he said,

> "Am I your father that you should pester me so?
> Neither pigeon, nor duck—nothing shall I forgo!
> You cannot reap where you have not sown!
> Go to the market place and buy your own!"

And the stranger was driven from the palace empty-handed.

Another year went by, and Atchanminanguey remained as prosperous as ever. His wives and children were in good health, and his orchard produced fruits of all kinds—mangos, guavas, oranges, papayas, and pineapples. His cattle were the envy of the whole kingdom; and on his farm, sheep, goats, chickens, ducks, pigeons, turkeys, and guinea fowl abounded.

But one day, as Atchanminanguey was preparing to eat lunch, yet another dusty and careworn stranger came to his palace and asked for a pigeon and a duck. Atchanminanguey could hardly contain his irritation and he thundered,

"You'll get neither pigeon nor duck from me,
Though they be as sand on the shore of the sea!
Three times I have shown you the door!
Mark my words! Come here no more!"

And the stranger was driven from the palace empty-handed.

As Atchanminanguey was returning to the dining room, he heard one of his servants running after him. "Your Royal Highness!" the man cried, "your orchard, your farm, your cattle have all vanished without a trace!"

Atchanminanguey grabbed the servant by the collar and shouted, "Pull yourself together and stop talking nonsense!" But then he felt the ground shake and move under his feet. Faintness overcame him, and he held onto the wall for support. When he came to, everything was gone—his gorgeous mansion, his wives and children, his servants—and he found himself once more a ragged peasant farmer hugging the wall of his shack.

Atchanminanguey rubbed his eyes again and again and pinched himself, but the terrible nightmare would not go away. The tattered clothes on his back, the hungry rumblings of his stomach, and the run-down shack he clutched at were as real as the ground under his feet and the sun blazing in the sky.

It was then that he realized that the beggar and the spirit were the same. And the words of his benefactor came back to him:

"I give you these without asking for anything in return, except that you sacrifice a pigeon and a duck for me every year." And he heard his own words denying the spirit's request three times:

> "You have come to the wrong place!
> Your presence in my palace is a disgrace!
> Neither pigeon nor duck shall I forgo!
> Mark well my words! Come here no more!"

Clasping his hands to his head, Atchanminanguey ran all the way to the spot where the spirit had first appeared. Leaning against a tree and crying, he begged the spirit to come back and give him a second chance.

Suddenly, the tall, lanky man dressed in spotless white appeared before him and said, "I have heard your lamentations, Atchanminanguey, but before I make you rich again, you must dance for me!" So speaking, the spirit started singing, beating his chest like a drum:

> "Come here, Atchanminanguey, and show me
> How well you dance the dance of Hardship.
> Come near, Atchanminanguey, and let me
> Watch you dance the dance of Poverty.
> You had ducks without number,
> But not one could you sacrifice for the spirit.
> You had pigeons beyond counting,

Yet not one could you spare for me.
Come here, Atchanminanguey, and show me
How well you dance the dance of Hardship.
Come near, Atchanminanguey, and let me
Watch you dance the dance of Poverty."

Atchanminanguey's despair turned to hope. Silently he vowed to show the spirit what a good dancer he was. He danced to the right, and he danced to the left. He danced forward, he danced backward, and he danced around and around. He danced until he was out of breath and drenched in sweat, and yet he went on dancing. He was still dancing when the spirit melted into thin air, never to reappear, leaving Atchanminanguey to keep dancing all by himself, with neither singer nor drummer, the dance of poverty.

In Fon culture, *gratitude to one's benefactor is very important, and so is keeping promises. In failing to sacrifice a pigeon and a duck to the spirit once a year, Atchanminanguey has violated two important moral laws. Far more serious, however, is his inability to give to the poor or to share with the needy. The sight of Atchanminanguey dancing all by himself with neither singer nor drummer signals his madness, which is the ultimate alienation. For in refusing to give, Atchanminanguey alienates himself, not only from his fellow human beings, but also from the spiritual world.*

The Greedy Father

Once upon a time, in a small village, there lived a man named Nadjo. He was wretchedly poor and lived in a crumbling shack. But he had a daughter, beautiful beyond compare, named Gbessi. She was tall and full-bodied, with big, bright eyes, a dazzling smile, and a complexion the color of copper. Nadjo could hardly wait until his daughter came of age for marriage, for when he looked at her, he could think of nothing but the bags of gold her beauty would bring him as a bride-price.

All the young men in the village were fascinated by Gbessi's beauty and wanted to marry her. Countless men, strong, hard-working, and handsome, came forward and requested her hand. Some brought half the provisions in their barns and lengths of fine fabric, but Nadjo was not satisfied.

Others brought all the provisions in their barns, fabrics, and jewelry. Still, Gbessi's father was not satisfied. None of the suitors was rich enough for the bride-price he had in mind. Being an obedient daughter, Gbessi turned down all the marriage proposals that were made to her. And, one after another, the suitors went away, humiliated and broken-hearted.

One day, a monkey living in the jungle heard about

Gbessi's matchless beauty and her father's greed. He was a very ugly monkey, but he was also very clever, and he decided he was going to marry the beautiful Gbessi. From the priceless cloths he had stolen, he made himself beautiful garments. Ant built him a beautiful house, while Dog, Lion, and Panther supplied him with plenty of meat. Elephant offered him firewood, Bee brought him honey, Hare brought him yams and cassava, and Partridge brought him millet and corn. Eagle gave him expensive necklaces and bangles, and Squirrel brought him gold and diamonds.

The generosity of Monkey's friends made him very wealthy indeed, and with his own magical powers he transformed himself into a handsome man. And so it was that Monkey set out for Gbessi's village, bearing expensive gifts and dressed up as a wealthy, good-looking young man.

As soon as Nadjo saw Monkey, his clothes and the gifts he had brought—the gorgeous fabrics, the priceless jewels, and the provisions—he was convinced he had found the ideal husband for his daughter. Gbessi herself found Monkey more handsome than all the men who had proposed to her, and she had no other wish than to marry him.

"I can see that you will make a wonderful husband for my daughter," Nadjo said, fingering the diamonds, the gold, and the jewels Monkey had laid out before him, "but you cannot marry my daughter unless you bring more provisions and bags of gold and diamonds."

Monkey's eyes widened in amazement at Nadjo's greed, but he quickly pulled himself together and said, "What I am offering you is but a token of my love, for your daughter is indeed beyond price. If you let me take your beautiful daughter with me, I will make you the happiest man on earth before the year is out." Nadjo had no reason to doubt Monkey's promise, and he gave his consent without further ado.

The wedding that followed was without parallel in living memory. People came from far and near in their best and most expensive clothes, but no one was more beautifully attired than Gbessi and her bridegroom. Food and drink were plentiful— palm wine and beer, rice and chicken or beef stew, pounded yam and bush meat soup, black-eye peas laced with palm oil, red corn paste—and there was much dancing and singing. Monkey showered singers and dancers alike, the best together with the worst, with gold coins.

At the close of the wedding ceremony, Gbessi set out with her handsome young husband for her new home. Every morning thereafter, Monkey and his wife would head to the new farm he had bought. And for a few months they lived happily, tilling the soil as farmers.

Monkey soon tired of his new life, however. He found the clothing of civilized man increasingly restrictive and the interminable days of hard work on the farm both boring and tiring beyond endurance for his monkey nature. He missed the company of the other monkeys. He missed swinging his way from one tree to another, frolicking and chattering all day long, or stealing food from neighboring farms and scampering off at the slightest sign of danger.

One day, while Gbessi and he were working the land in preparation for the planting season, Monkey suddenly threw his hoe down in disgust, and moving away from his wife, he uttered a few magical words. And lo! He turned back into a monkey! Gbessi heard her husband mumble and, turning to ask what he had said, saw not her husband but a hideous monkey discarding his man-made garments. The monkey's tail was still missing, but Gbessi watched in utter amazement as it grew back.

She stood paralyzed on the spot. Then it occurred to her that she had married not a young and wealthy man, but a hideous monkey. Uttering a piercing cry, she broke into a run. Monkey ran after her in hot pursuit, driven by anger and fear of being found out.

Gbessi was a fast runner, and she ran as swiftly as her legs could carry her. She leapt over fallen tree trunks, gaping holes and ditches, streams and boulders, uprooting the grass that got entangled with her feet. But Monkey gained steadily upon her, for he was native to the jungle and knew many a shortcut through its paths and thickets.

Soon Gbessi could feel Monkey's hot breath on her back. At that moment, however, her native village appeared in the distance, and she knew salvation was at hand. Marshalling her breath and increasing her speed, Gbessi put a few yards between herself and her pursuer. But as she ran through the gate to her father's compound, crying, "Father, help me! Father, save me!" Monkey made a giant leap forward and tapped her on the shoulder.

Nadjo, who had rushed out of his house upon hearing his daughter's cry for help, saw the beauteous Gbessi transformed into a monkey before his very eyes. Her hair coarsened and stiffened and spread all over her body. Her graceful limbs withered, her shining eyes glitterd with monkey cunning, and, making a grimace, she turned away from her heartbroken father to her new home in the jungle.

Within days, Nadjo went mad with grief and the guilt of his own greed, and died shortly thereafter.

"He or she who marries *a stranger may be exposing himself or herself to terrible danger." That warning, which is a commonplace of traditional African culture, finds expression in this tale. What makes this story one of the most interesting in Beninese and African folklore, however, is that it captures the metamorphosis motif in African literature, a motif that goes to the heart of the African colonial experience. Ngugi Wa Thiong'o, the great Kenyan writer, uses a variant of "The Greedy Father" in a short story entitled "A Meeting in the Dark," one of the most eloquent fictional accounts of the African colonial experience.*

When
The
River
Becomes
The
"Big Hole"

Long ago, when beasts were still gifted with the power of speech, two peasant women from a village in the forest were hurrying back home from their cornfields one evening. The sun had gone down over the rim of the horizon, and the shadows of night were fast spreading over the earth, rousing in the hearts of men and women alike fear of ghosts, witches, and beasts. Except for the crickets chirping in the underbrush and a few birds slowly winging their way across the somber sky, the two women had only each other for company. Yet, there was no fear in their voices as they pressed their way homeward in the gathering darkness, chatting merrily as they walked.

A lone hyena prowling about in the shadows heard their voices and perked up his ears, for there was no knowing what secrets would get mixed up in the chatter of women trying to kill time. He didn't have long to wait, for as the houses of the village loomed into view and the two women were about to part company, one said to the other, "Adononsi, do not forget we have to go down to the river to fetch water before sunrise tomorrow. . . . I will knock on your door at the first light of dawn.

. . . Sleep is your favorite friend, I know . . . but don't let me knock twice when I come for you."

"Don't talk as if you don't know me, Adjoua. You are the one who can't get enough of sleep," the other woman retorted, slapping her thigh to give emphasis to her words. "I will be picking my teeth and laughing when you finally drag yourself to my doorstep, for everyone would have come back from the river and forgotten about it."

A brief exchange of good-humored gibes followed amid much thigh-slapping, and then the two friends took leave of each other.

Hyena shadowed one of them until he found out where she lived. Then he slunk away, grinning from ear to ear and muttering gleefully, "Don't let me knock twice when I come for you."

In the dead of night, while the whole village was asleep, Hyena made a towering pile of firewood near the marketplace and set it alight. And while the mound of sticks and twigs was engulfed in flames and a soft twilight radiance spread over the village, he dressed up as a woman and went knocking on Adononsi's door: "Adononsi! Adononsi! Get up and let's go! The sun is about to rise, and we must hurry!"

"What? Daybreak already?" Adononsi yawned, rising stiffly to her feet and rubbing her eyes vigorously to shake off the sleep clinging to them. "Let me get dressed and we will be on our way," she went on, opening the door. "You really are an early riser, there is no doubt about it."

"I told you I was going to beat you to it, but you wouldn't listen," Hyena said, imitating Adjoua's voice, and keeping out of sight.

Adononsi found her friend's voice a little raspy but didn't think much of it. Her friend was distant, but Adononsi thought it was because she was upset. Adononsi got dressed, washed her face, put a chewing-stick into her mouth to clean her breath, and set out for the river, followed by her companion.

The air was unusually chilly, and the radiance that had lighted their path as they set out gradually dimmed to darkness. The village roosters, who always greeted every new dawn with a chorus of "Kokorioko" were silent, and there was not a soul in sight. Adononsi found the silence all the more unsettling because her companion hadn't opened her mouth once since they left home.

"I find it strange that it is getting darker, not lighter, and that not a single rooster has crowed so far," Adononsi said in an attempt to break the silence.

"I don't know why it is getting darker, not lighter, or why no rooster has crowed so far," Hyena answered sharply, quickening his pace and breathing down Adononsi's neck.

It was then that Adononsi suspected something was horribly wrong and turned around to take a close look at her companion. What she saw was not Adjoua her friend, but a beast casting away women's clothing. Adononsi looked desperately for a way out of the trap into which she had fallen, pressing her hands to her throat to keep from screaming, lest Hyena know he had been found out.

"Adjoua," she said at last, "I need to step into the bush for a few moments. I have got to answer a call of nature . . . I can't help myself. . . . Please. . . . I won't be long."

"You'd better not keep me waiting," Hyena growled, stamping his feet, his hair standing on end, his eyes gleaming with malice.

Quickly Adononsi slipped into the bush and, taking cover behind a clump of trees, put her loincloth and her headscarf over a stout, jagged stick rooted to the ground. Then she fled as fast as her feet could carry her.

In the meantime Hyena was waiting, crouching low in the middle of the path, his claws at the ready, his teeth flashing. Soon his patience wore thin, and he took to pacing up and down the path, wondering why on earth Adononsi had kept him waiting so long. Then, unable to contain his anger any longer, he tore through the forest until he reached what he thought was Adononsi hiding behind a clump of trees. Propelled by a seething rage, Hyena leaped high in the air and came crashing down to his death upon the stick Adononsi had dressed up as herself.

The news of Adononsi's narrow escape from the trap set by Hyena spread with amazing speed through the village and to the four corners of the region. And so it was that the belief came to prevail among the people that it was not safe to discuss a trip or a journey at night. To this day, when villagers have to tell someone they will go to the river to draw water at dawn, they say they will be going down to the "Big Hole."

Among the Fon, *it is taboo to call someone by name aloud or to discuss a trip at night. Although that custom is dying out in the city, it retains much of its power in rural areas, where fear of evil spirits and witches makes people call each other by false names at night if they cannot hold their voices down. It is not uncommon for people to call each other "Bird," "Tree," "River," or "Cow" when they call to each other at night. This story dramatizes the dangers to which the two women expose themselves in discussing so openly at night their trip to the river the next day.*

Can You Save The Day?

Once upon a time, in a village on the shore of the mighty Zou River, there was a maiden named Adononsi, beautiful beyond any singing of it. She was a woman of majestic bearing, tall and straight, with a complexion of shining ebony and big, flashing eyes. She had many friends, but among these, three were dear to her above all others, three young men gifted with magical powers. With three secret magical words, one could make his sight so keen as to see over great distances, through shadowy jungles and towering mountains. Another had a shoe that could turn into a canoe swifter than a hawk swooping down upon a chick, and the third was so strong he could lift a gigantic baobab tree high into the air with his little finger.

Where Adononsi and these three young men lived, many a strong and wonderful friendship had drawn popular praise and aroused much envy, but theirs was the strongest and the most wonderful of all. Within its magic circle, conflict was unknown. No sacrifice was too great to make, and no gift was too much to give. Perfect harmony held sway among the friends.

One day, Adononsi decided to go on a journey to visit relatives. The village was far away, and few women would dare travel the distance alone, but Adononsi was strong and fearless.

"It is a long, long journey, with many a wild beast and evil spirit lying in wait for the unwary," her three friends told her. "Let us keep you company, for there is no knowing what trouble you may get into."

"There is neither beast nor spirit more fearsome than fear," Adononsi replied. "I will be back in seven days from now, safe and sound." Adononsi sounded so confident and so determined that her friends had to let her go.

Two days after she was gone, however, the three friends were awakened at dawn by loud, desperate knocks on their door, and a hysterical voice calling, "Help! Help! My daughter is missing! Help!" It was Adononsi's father, and what he told them struck fear into their hearts. Two whole days had gone by since Adononsi set out on her journey, and yet she still had not reached her destination. Her relatives had sent out search parties, but she was nowhere to be found! Adononsi had vanished without a trace, and there was no knowing what danger had befallen her!

The far-seeing man immediately pronounced the secret magic words and lo! Far, far away, in a jungle bordering the southernmost reaches of the Zou River, he saw a terrible sight: The rainbow snake, the father of all snakes and giver of riches, had taken Adononsi captive. He had put her in a big hole in the ground and had covered it with his gigantic head. He wanted Adononsi to marry him and had promised her untold wealth, but she would not give her consent. The rainbow snake would stop at nothing to have his way and was threatening to kill Adononsi at any moment.

It was common knowledge that when the rainbow snake took a fancy to a woman and carried her away to his realm against her will, she was almost beyond help. And even if she managed to escape, no power on earth could stop the rainbow snake from coming after her. The only way she could repel him would be to find a husband right away. Adononsi was indeed in deep trouble.

Quick as the wind, the man with the magic shoe rushed to the shore of the river, his two companions following close behind. He threw his magic shoe into the water, and soon the three friends were seated in a canoe speeding down the Zou River.

Theirs was the fastest canoe on the face of the earth, but the lair of the rainbow snake was far, far away. They paddled and paddled, through violent storms and mighty whirlwinds, until their arms felt numb. They paddled all day long, and yet they seemed no closer.

Suddenly, at a bend in the river, behind a screen of tall and leafy trees, they glimpsed a blaze of yellow, red, blue, and green. The rainbow snake, the father of all snakes, was within sight, and the battle that would decide their friend's fate was at hand.

Nimble as a cat, the man gifted with superhuman strength jumped ashore and stealthily made his way into the jungle, his heart pounding. He had not gone very far when he came upon the rainbow snake, coiled around a massive, towering tree. The splendid, many-colored skin of the snake was like a thousand mirrors held to the sun. All the snakes of the earth put together would not be half as big as he. His tail was hidden from view in the topmost branches of the tree, while his gigantic head lay on the ground, blocking a wide hole where Adononsi was held captive.

Quiet as a shadow, the man crept up to the edge of the

hole. Then, holding his breath, he lifted the snake's colossal head slowly, ever so gently, with one finger. The rainbow snake felt something soft tickle him on the throat, and he wriggled his neck to shake off what he thought was an ant. Adononsi's friend felt faint with fear, but he was not a man easily cowed by danger. "I will fight the rainbow snake if I have to," he thought to himself, as he silently helped Adononsi out of the hole.

But he did not have to fight, for it had not occurred to the rainbow snake that any creature of flesh and blood would dare to come between him and his prisoner. And while the rainbow snake was deep in thought, searching for a way to win over the most beautiful woman ever to have walked the earth, Adononsi and her rescuer stole their way back to the magic canoe.

With the other two young men, they returned home to a rapturous welcome. Men, women, and children came out to greet them, singing and dancing; a great feast was held to give thanks for Adononsi's safe return and to honor the three young men who had combined their magical powers to rescue their friend from captivity.

At the height of the feast, while mouthfuls of delicious, spicy food were being washed down with palm wine and Adononsi's house echoed with the jokes and good cheer of a thousand guests, a dispute broke out among the three friends who had joined in Adononsi's rescue.

The one who was gifted with supernatural strength was seen rising to his feet, his eyes blazing, his right hand jabbing at the air in an impassioned argument with his two friends. "I am the one who lifted the rainbow snake's head," he barked. "I am the one who helped our friend out of the hole. I must claim Adononsi as my wife, for I have done more than both of you to save her."

The one who provided the magic canoe jumped up, as if stung by a scorpion, and cried: "Your superhuman strength would have availed nothing, nor would Adononsi have lived to tell the tale, had it not been for my magic canoe. I, not you, deserve to take her to wife."

"What about me!" the far-seeing man exclaimed, beating his chest to give emphasis to his claim. "With all your superhuman strength and your magic canoe, you would have roamed the earth in vain, had I not found the rainbow snake out, or told you where Adononsi lay trapped in a hole, staring death in the face. If anyone deserves to be given her hand in marriage, surely I must be the one."

The three friends would have come to blows if the dispute had not been referred to the council of elders. But even they, with all their wisdom, were unable to decide who should be given Adononsi's hand in marriage. It was then that Adononsi herself was brought in to settle the matter. But Adononsi was not herself that day. Her self-confidence, her strength, and her sparkle seemed to have deserted her as she held her three friends in her gaze and looked from one to another, again and again, her eyes glistening with tears. Then, she shook her head, and tears came trickling down her cheeks as her beautiful, haunting voice rang out in song:

"Woe is me! Woe is me! I know not whom to choose!
I cannot decide who must gain and who must lose!

The rainbow snake took me away to his home,
Where neither humans nor beasts ever roam.
'Be my beloved,' he said, 'or breathe your last.'
Friends of my youth, in your gifts I was blessed!

The rainbow snake has golden jewels and rubies.
Friends of my youth! You're far greater than these!

But now you're at strife, and friendship is no more,
I have become the poorest among the earth's poor.

Woe is me! Woe is me! I know not whom to choose.
I cannot decide who must gain and who must lose!"

As the three young men stood listening, there came to them a vision of the soul of their friendship wounded to death and weeping aloud over her great misfortune. The surge of anger that had made them turn on one another ebbed away to sadness, and they bowed their heads.

Drawing apart from the gathering, they asked the elders' permission for a few moments' consultation. Then they announced their decision: They would give Adononsi and the elders as much time as was needed to find a solution. And until it was decided who among them should be given Adononsi's hand in marriage, they would move heaven and earth to keep her safe from the rainbow snake.

That very night, word went forth to the four corners of the land for advice on how to settle the most difficult matter ever to defy the wisdom of the elders. To this day, the council of elders has been waiting. Adononsi is still without a husband, and time is running out. The rainbow snake may come at any moment, but Adononsi's friends have vowed to fight him to the death. Violence and bloodshed must be prevented at all costs, and that is why I have come to tell this tale.

Who knows? One of you may succeed where the council of elders has failed. Can you save the day?

The python, *called* Dangbe, *is one of the gods in the Fon pantheon. And the rainbow, called* Aido Houedo, *is venerated as a* *giver of wealth in Fon culture. This is the only Fon story I have heard where* Aido Houedo *or any animal or spirit carries off a woman in an attempt to marry her. "Can You Save the Day?" is designed to test the wisdom of listeners and to spark a debate about a problem that has no obvious or easy solution. Whatever the individual merits of the three friends who combined their magical powers in rescuing Adononsi, none could be said to have played a lesser role than another.*

The inability of the council of elders to decide who among the three friends should marry the woman signals the difficulty of the problem. But the most important point of the story, perhaps, is that nothing lasts forever and that even the closest friendships come under strain sometimes.

The Girl Who Brought the Rainy Season And the Dry Season

My story takes flight and, soaring through the mists of time to the beginning of the world, alights in a village where once there lived a little girl, Agossi, and her widowed mother, Agossinon. Agossi had a radiant complexion, a graceful neck, and a dimple that made her smile the most beautiful smile on the face of the earth. She was her mother's only child and was dearer to her than the very breath of life. But she was also her despair, for Agossi simply could not hold her tongue, in spite of her mother's repeated warnings:

> "If you see a tree with roots where leaves should have been,
> Or fish that is black, white, yellow, blue, red, and green,
> Hold your tongue, child, for you may have seen a spirit.
>
> If you see a man with his eyes at the back of his head,
> Or a pregnant woman carrying the little one in her neck,
> Hold your tongue, child, for you may have seen a spirit.
>
> If you see a newborn with the teeth of a full-grown man,
> Or a person with a thousand and one toes instead of ten,
> Hold your tongue, child, for you may have seen a spirit."

Agossinon's warnings were wasted breath. Whatever her daughter's eyes saw would set words rolling off her tongue, and there was nothing Agossinon could do about it.

One day, Agossi saw her mother preparing for a journey and said, "Mother, I want to go with you."

"This is not a journey for you," her mother replied, "for it is a very long journey with many a strange sight along the way to tempt the unwary to their ruin."

"I want to go with you," Agossi whimpered, hanging her head. "I promise not to breathe a word no matter how strange the sights I see along the way."

"I fear your tongue will outrun your resolution and land you in terrible danger," Agossinon said, "for there is many a strange sight along the way to tempt the unwary to their doom. Stay home, child, for I fear your journey may be a journey of no return."

Agossi burst out crying, and tears came streaming down her cheeks. The sight of her daughter's beautiful face bathed in tears pained Agossinon beyond endurance. So she said, "I will take you with me, but you must promise to keep silent, even if you see a man with his head growing beneath his shoulders."

"I have given you my word already," Agossi sobbed. "I will not breathe a single word, even if I see a man with *three* heads growing beneath his shoulders."

Agossinon made Agossi swear a vow of silence, and soon mother and daughter set out on the long journey with many a strange sight along the way to tempt the unwary to their deaths.

They walked and walked until all familiar sights and sounds faded away, and still they walked, Agossinon following behind her daughter on the narrow, winding path. Not a bird song was to be heard, not a breath of wind stirred the grass, and the trees stood gaunt and motionless. As the sun hung high in the sky, they came to the edge of a field, where a flea was tilling the soil with a hoe in preparation for the planting season.

Agossi's mouth fell wide open, and pointing at the flea, she cried, "A flea wielding a hoe! This is a strange sight indeed! Who would have thought there was so much strength in such tiny arms! A strange sight indeed!"

No sooner had Agossi spoken those words, than her mother saw her change into a flea before her very eyes. Agossinon felt numb all over. Clasping both hands to her head, she broke into lamentations, weeping, begging, and singing for the spirit to have mercy:

"Agossi my child, look what you have got yourself into!
I gave you warning, but my warning did not get through!
If you see a flea tilling a field,
Hold your tongue, child, for you may have seen a spirit."

Agossinon wept so bitterly and sang so movingly that the spirit restored Agossi to her, and the two travelers went on their way.

They walked until the sun started going down, and still they walked. Suddenly, there came into view a river glistening white and flowing upstream. Agossi held her breath and clasped her hands to her mouth a moment, visibly struggling to keep a tight rein on her tongue. But in the end, the words came spilling out: "Mother, my playmates will think I am mad if I tell them I have seen a river of milk flowing upstream! I have seen a flea wielding a hoe and thought it was a very strange sight, but this really is beyond belief!"

No sooner were those words out of her mouth, than a crocodile came splashing out of the waters and dragged Agossi down beneath the milky waves.

Once again Agossinon clasped her hands to her head and, dropping to her knees, broke into lamentations, weeping, begging, and singing for the spirit to have mercy:

"Agossi my child, look what you have got yourself into!
I gave you warning, but my warning did not get through!
If you see a flea tilling a field,
Hold your tongue, child, for you may have seen a spirit.
If you see a river glistening white and flowing upstream,
Hold your tongue, child, for you may have seen a spirit."

Again, Agossinon wept so bitterly and sang so movingly that the crocodile released her daughter, and soon Agossi and Agossinon resumed their journey. The sun had all but vanished from sight, touching the horizon with fire when, at a bend in the path, the two travelers came upon a skeleton holding its head in one hand and scooping water from a calabash with the other. It was Death washing itself.

Agossi's eyes came bulging out, and she stood, petrified. Then, burying her face in her hands, she cried, "Mother, this is a strange sight indeed! I have seen a flea tilling a field, and a river of milk flowing upstream, but this makes them both look like mere trifles! A skeleton clutching its head in one hand and scooping water from a calabash with the other! This is a very strange sight indeed!"

Agossi's mother gestured wildly as though struggling to capture her daughter's words and trample them into the dust, but the girl's words were past recalling. Quick as an arrow, Death aimed its skull at Agossi and struck her dead.

Agossinon's blood ran cold as she clasped her hands to her head and broke into lamentations, begging, weeping, and singing for Death to have mercy and restore her daughter to her:

"Agossi my child, look what you have got yourself into!
I gave you warning, but my warning did not get through!
If you see a flea tilling a field,

Hold your tongue, child, for you may have seen a spirit.
If you see a river glistening white and flowing upstream,
Hold your tongue, child, for you may have seen a spirit.
If you see a skeleton holding his skull in his hand,
Hold your tongue, child, for you may have seen Death."

But Death took no notice. She dropped to her knees, tore her shirt to shreds, weeping, pleading, and singing for Death to have mercy and return her daughter to her, but Death stopped his ears.

Still, Agossinon would not give up. She rolled in the dust, tearing her hair out by its roots, weeping, begging, and singing for Death to give her daughter one more chance.

Agossinon wept so forlornly and sang so movingly that Death, at last, was touched with compassion, for he had never seen as much grief as Agossinon had expressed over her daughter's death. And he said in a dry, skeletal voice that sent chills down Agossinon's spine, "Weep no more, Agossinon. Wipe your tears and listen. I have glad tidings for you. Rather than keep your daughter to myself for evermore, I will allow her to spend half her time with you. . . . But do not try to keep her from coming back to me when her time is up, for if you do, there will be trouble."

The earth shook, flashes of lightening crisscrossed the sky, and Death vanished from sight, taking Agossi with him. But he kept his word, for a few months after he took Agossi away, he allowed her to spend an equal amount of time with her mother on condition she would reveal no secrets of the country of the dead.

And so it was that Agossi found herself dividing her time between the world of the living and the world of the dead. For the duration of her stay in the country of the dead, her mother would weep bitterly, and whenever she wept, the sky would cover itself with dark clouds, and rain would pour down upon the earth amid flashes of lightening and claps of thunder. To ease her grief, Agossi's mother would keep herself busy by tilling the land and growing crops. Sometimes, she would remember a song she used to sing with her daughter, and she would weep most bitterly and would not be comforted. At these moments, it would rain harder than ever, and rivers would burst their banks, burying vast expanses of land under water.

When it was time for her daughter to come for a visit, however, Agossinon would gather in the yield of her farm, and deck herself out in fine clothes and glittering jewels. Throughout her daughter's sojourn, Agossinon's joy would know no bounds, and there would be much feasting and rejoicing all over the land. In the daytime, the sun would burn bright, and at night the moon and the stars would spread a magical radiance over the earth.

Sometimes, Agossinon would find her daughter's presence such a delight that she would try to keep her longer than allowed. And whenever Agossi was made to stay beyond her time, the sun would blaze fiercely in the heavens, burning the earth. Nor would the ensuing drought cease until Agossinon let her daughter go.

Throughout Agossi's visit, her mother, her relatives, and her playmates would keep asking her, "What are things like on the other side?" But Agossi would only smile and say, "That I cannot tell you . . . it must remain a secret." And they would shake their heads in amazement, for the impossible had come to pass—Agossi had learned to hold her tongue, at long last. That is why, to this day, no one knows for sure what happens to people when they pass out of this world to the Great Beyond.

This variant of the story of Persephone in Greek mythology is a story to which I have made a few significant contributions. The original tale ends with Death carrying off the girl who could not hold her tongue. In my adaptation, however, Death is moved to compassion by the mother's pleas and decides to allow the girl to spend half the year in the world of the living. Thus, a cautionary tale warning children against indiscretion and impulsiveness, and encouraging them to reserve judgment, becomes as well a story explaining the origin of the seasons. Furthermore, it dramatizes the Fon concept of the interconnectedness of life and death. Among the Fon, death is considered the other side of life, and the dead are considered spirits that must be propitiated through libations and other ceremonies.

In adapting the story, I drew not only upon my knowledge of the Persephone tale but also upon my experience of bereavement. Between 1990 and 1994, I lost two people who were very dear to me: my friend Fayad and my sister Rafath. One of the things I learned as I mourned them was that death was not a final separation and that there were times when our loved ones who had crossed over to the Great Beyond would come back to keep us company. "The Girl Who Brought the Rainy Season and the Dry Season" is therefore a crossbreed born of the combination of an ancient folktale with Western mythology and personal experience.

The King Who Would Be God

Once upon a time, there was a king. He was a whale of a man, tall and massive, with a chest like the trunk of an iroko tree, the legs of a giant, and a voice like the rumbling of distant thunder. He boasted that ten men linking hands could not encircle his torso, and people believed him. He had named himself "The Mountain That Cannot Be Moved" and wielded absolute power over his subjects. He had subdued all his enemies in war and was feared throughout his realm. His whims and his will alike were law, and no one could contradict him or incur his displeasure and live.

This arrogant king was a self-proclaimed Christian and an assiduous churchgoer. He attended church in the morning and in the evening, wearing garments of silk and brocade, a crown of gold, necklaces and bangles of silver studded with diamonds and emeralds, and shoes of matchless craftsmanship. His entrances and exits were marked by all the members of the congregation bowing down before him and rubbing their foreheads in the dust.

One day, The Mountain That Cannot Be Moved demanded to know the meaning of a song that the congregation was particularly fond of singing. It was a beautiful song, and it echoed sweetly in his ears, but it was an old song in an ancient language. And when he asked the worshippers what the song meant, no one could tell him. So The Mountain That Cannot Be Moved summoned the priest and requested a translation of the hymn.

"This song is in praise of the Lord," the priest observed, "but what it says is nothing new. It pays tribute to God as the greatest of all kings, the king whose kingdom encompasses heaven and earth, and whose rule has no beginning and no end. It bears witness to the glory and the majesty of the king whose power passes all understanding and compared to whom all other kings are mere worms crawling in the dust. Ah, this song. . . ."

"Enough!" the king thundered. "What king is more powerful than The Mountain That Cannot Be Moved?" he rumbled, rising up on his gigantic feet and surveying the cowering congregation, his chest rising and falling like a ship in stormy seas. "The king is not born who will not quake in his shoes at the mere mention of my name! I would have all of you beheaded one by one for taking my name in vain, if your ignorance were not so laughable! But let that song be silenced out of existence now and forever more, for no one can sing it and live. Such is my will, and such it will remain. Should anyone doubt my resolve, come to church tomorrow and see how swiftly my wrath will smite those who trespass against the law!" Having spoken thus, the king stormed out, ignoring the congregation's bows and gestures of self-abasement.

The next day was Sunday, and The Mountain That Cannot Be Moved went to church and made his entrance with the usual pomp. Halfway through the service, as though impelled by a power beyond their will, the congregation broke into song, and the words of the forbidden song, words of praise and thanksgiving, came rolling off their tongues. While it lasted, the song bore the congregation aloft, spiritually lifting its members high above all earthly cares. Their fears and sorrows, their dread of the king and his threat of instant and overwhelming retribution were as dead leaves in the storm of holy fervor that had laid hold of them.

When the song ended, the congregation, as if suddenly realizing that it had broken the king's edict, looked around in fear. But no fire overwhelmed them, and no thunderbolt struck them! They had sung the very song the king had prohibited under pain of death, and he took no action!

What prevented the swift descent of the king's wrath upon them was indeed a miracle. But it was not the miraculous change of heart they had imagined. God had heard the vain and boastful words of The Mountain That Cannot Be Moved, and God had acted. God commanded one of his angels to make himself into a likeness of the king. Then God changed the appearance of The Mountain That Cannot Be Moved beyond recognition. While God did this, the look-alike angel-king slipped onto the throne.

So it was that shortly after his arrival in church, The Mountain That Cannot Be Moved was transformed into a ragged, unshaven tramp and put to sleep in a far corner. No human eye had witnessed the sudden and mysterious change God had wrought.

Long after the service was over and everyone had gone home, there came from within the church a knocking, loud enough to wake the dead, and an angry voice shouted hysterically in the dark, "Let me out! Let me out! How dare you lock me in like a homeless urchin, a common vagrant! Let me out

now before I break the door down and tear you all to pieces
with my own hands!"

Roused from sleep, the sexton shuffled to the gate and un-
locked it. "Who is it?" he asked, thrusting his lamp close to the
gaunt face that loomed before him.

"Who am I indeed!" The Mountain That Cannot Be
Moved shrieked, sweeping past and raining curses both on him
and all those who had so insulted their majesty.

The sexton stared after the ragged fellow. Concluding finally that some madman had fallen asleep in church and been
accidentally locked in, the sexton crossed himself and went back
to his post.

Later that night, the guards at the palace were equally startled when a hysterical voice pierced the still night air, threatening to execute everybody. They saw an elephantine figure
dressed in rags come charging up, calling them by name and
commanding them to unbar the gates at once, cursing and
swearing. The guards looked at each other, amazed, and wondered who this man was who knew them by name and who
claimed to be their king.

"What madness has come over you!" The Mountain That
Cannot Be Moved cried. "What evil spirit has turned your
heads! Do you not see me! Ah! you have eyes, and yet you do
not see! You have ears, yet you do not hear me! I am the king,
The Mountain That Cannot Be Moved! Open the gates before I
kill you one by one." And the intruder banged on the gates and
made such a racket that he had to be bound and locked up in a
room where sleep finally put an end to his ranting and raving.

The guards speculated far into the night about the madman. What they had seen was not their king, but a ragged, unshaven, foul-mouthed tramp who had gone soft in the head. Of

the miraculous change that God had wrought upon their king and the divine purpose behind it, they knew nothing at all.

In the morning, the guards told the angel-king about the tramp, and the angel-king ordered him to be brought out. Although he was much more subdued than the night before, The Mountain That Cannot Be Moved argued passionately that he was the true king, calling the ancestors and God to witness. But all his arguing was in vain.

No one believed him. His wives recoiled from him and laughed cruel, nervous laughs when he called them by their names and said he was their husband. His own sons and daughters thought him mad when he addressed them as his own children.

Clearly he was out of his mind, and his knowledge of names was put down to trickery. Someone suggested he was a mad court jester with the gift of clairvoyance. So, from then on, everyone called him "the mad court jester," and his claim to be the king, and all of the strange things he said or did, were interpreted as mad jokes. Everyone was amazed when the angel-king provided this crazy fellow with a room and commanded all members of the royal household, and all his subjects, to treat him kindly.

For days and nights together, The Mountain That Cannot Be Moved mulled over his fall from king to court jester, but no matter how he looked at it, he couldn't comprehend it.

"How on earth did this thing happen?" he wondered. "Who can tell me by what power I, The Mountain That Cannot Be Moved, a powerful king, have become a mad court jester, a laughingstock?" he asked himself over and over again. And over and over he rubbed his eyes, expecting to awake from his nightmare and find himself once again firmly seated on his throne. But that was a forlorn hope.

Time passed. The people had known their king as a despot and a bully, but now he seemed a caring and compassionate monarch. Poverty, hunger, and disease were banished from the kingdom. Crime was punished, virtue was rewarded, and justice, tempered by mercy, prevailed.

Commerce flourished once again, bringing great wealth and prosperity. Ships came from all over the world, laden with spices, expensive cloths, and tapestries, gold and gems; and they went away bearing palm oil, cotton, cassava, and carvings of unparalleled workmanship. Christianity spread, new converts swelled its ranks daily, and no one was more devoted to its cause than the king.

People wondered at the miraculous change that had come over the king. Some attributed it to his regular attendance at church services. Others suggested that the king, like Jacob in the Bible, was challenged to a fight by the spirit of God one moonless night and had not been the same ever since. All his subjects were deeply mystified. But of their true king's transfiguration into a mad court jester and the divine purpose behind it, they knew nothing at all.

The mad court jester, too, saw the angel-king's righteousness, compassion, and love. He saw his humility and his wisdom. He saw the peace and the prosperity he had brought to the people. Like the others, he was inclined to praise the king, even though his own fall from power was beyond his understanding.

One night, he had a dream. He saw himself seated on the throne and wearing a crown of gold. But instead of courtiers and royal grandees, he was surrounded by a throng of wailing orphans and widows, cripples and beggars, lepers and epileptics, all tugging at his garments, beseeching him for help. His shouts and his threats alike were powerless to hold them back and soon his royal attire was reduced to rags, the very rags he was wearing the night he awoke, a beggar and a madman, in church.

Then, the dream changed, and he found himself in the company of thieves, murderers, and evildoers. The air rang with their praises. They carried him shoulder-high and offered him a robe of lace and a crown of gold. But when he put these on, behold, the robe turned to rags, and the crown of gold changed into a crown of worms.

There was yet another change of dream-scenery, and the king found himself in church. The congregation was singing in praise of God, and he had decided to carry out his ominous threat of mass execution. But as he rose to give his soldiers the order, there was a blinding flash of lightning. The congregation and the soldiers alike vanished, and he found himself, a tramp dressed in rags, pounding on the doors of a dark and deserted church and clamoring to be let out.

The king woke up with a start, his heart racing furiously, his body drenched in sweat. The sun had risen. Voices raised in song or laughter, the joyous chatter of children at play, the twittering of birds, the beating of drums, and the tolling of church bells reached him faintly. All of those sounds spoke of a world from which he felt estranged, a world that had taken no notice of his fall from power.

Holding his head in both hands, The Mountain That Cannot Be Moved wept as he had never wept before, for he stood revealed to himself as he had appeared to his subjects: arrogant,

blind, and heartless, he had been a friend to the rich and powerful and an enemy to the poor, the sick, and the elderly.

Overwhelmed by a feeling that was new to him, he broke
into song:

"Woe is me! Woe is me! I ate sour oranges
And my teeth are set on edge!
I spoke words foul and boastful, and behold!
They turned to rocks and crushed my feet!
O Lord, have mercy!
When a king, I turned my hand against my people.
I sided with thieves, murderers,
And evildoers against the innocent.
I robbed the poor, denied food to the hungry,
Succor to the helpless,
And solace to the orphan and the widow.
O Lord, have mercy!
Woe is me! Woe is me! I ate sour oranges
And my teeth are set on edge!
I spoke words ungodly and blasphemous.
Behold! they turned to sharp blades
And slashed my mouth from ear to ear!
Harken to my supplications, O Lord!
Wash me clean of my sins,
And make your face shine upon me,
Lest I should stumble and fall yet again!"

That song became a prayer to him, and whenever he sang it, in
the morning or in the evening, all who heard him would pause
and listen, for it stirred something deep within them.

People marveled at the change that had come over him.
And, suddenly, as though by a common impulse, the members

of the royal household and all those who knew him started calling him "Man of God," and his former name, "the mad court jester," was forgotten.

One night, at the midnight hour, Man of God was deep in prayer when his room was flooded with light and an angel, brighter than a thousand suns, called out and bade him look him in the face.

"I cannot look you in the face," Man of God cried, shielding his eyes from the brilliant glitter that radiated from the four corners of his room. And the holy angel called him again by his name and spoke thus:

"Can a vessel of clay do battle with a vessel of brass and prevail, or a king of flesh and blood challenge the Holy King to a fight and win?

"The vessel of clay that wrestles with the vessel of brass, it shall be broken up into pieces; and the king who would be God, he shall be struck down into the dust.

"For the Lord's weakness is mightier than the combined might of all the armies of the earth, and his foolishness wiser than the accumulated wisdom of the ages.

"When their hour is spent, the king and the conqueror alike shall lie in the dust, with worms for a cover, for dust they are, and to dust they shall return. Fame, glory, and wealth— these shall pass like the flower of the field, but His Glory and His Kingdom shall never end.

"The flesh and all it hankers after will pass and leave not a trace behind. But Faith, Hope, and Love—they abide forever, and the greatest of these is Love.

"Go back to your family, go back to your people, and sin no more."

There was a flash of lightning, followed by a clap of thunder, and the angel disappeared. The room was plunged into darkness, and Man of God remained on his knees with his eyes closed; when he reopened them, behold, he was seated on his throne, dressed in garments of brocade, and wearing a crown of gold.

In the morning, Man of God, the former mad court jester, was nowhere to be found. The members of the royal household and those who knew him asked the king about him, and the king told them he had gone back where he came from, and they believed him. But of the miraculous change the holy angel had wrought upon their true king, and the divine purpose behind it, they knew nothing at all.

This story has *strong Christian overtones, but then Christianity was introduced to Benin about a century and a half ago. This story was told on Benin's national radio in the mid-1980s, the twilight years of a dictatorial regime that ruled the country from 1972 to 1990. At its worst, General Kerekou's regime was associated with gross human rights violations and corruption.*

Kerekou's regime resented the criticism leveled at it by various religious authorities. The discontinuation of the public broadcasting of Christian and Islamic religious services for many years was a thinly disguised retaliatory measure against what the regime saw as the interference of religion in politics. At a time when the regime had driven much of the opposition underground, the church stood as an outspoken critic of political oppression, police brutality, corruption, and injustice in the country.

In 1990, however, Kerekou reluctantly convened a na-

tional conference in the face of mounting economic problems, labor unrest, and pressure from various opposition groups. This conference paved the way for a transitional government, which organized democratic elections in March 1991. Kerekou was voted out of power, and a new government led by Nicephore Soglo was assembled. This was a milestone in modern African history, for it was the first time a dictator was voted out of power.

From 1991 to 1996, Kerekou remained in the political wilderness. But little by little, he achieved a resurgence of popularity as more and more people came to appreciate his humility and foresight in bowing out gracefully, thereby sparing the country a civil war.

When Kerekou was elected president in 1996 by the very people who had voted him out five years earlier, he declared that he would rule the country as a Christian. History will judge the truth or falsehood of his words, but the story of the king who would be God parallels to some extent Kerekou's rise and fall and resurgence. And through that story we catch a distant glimpse of the timelessness and the prophetic power of the storyteller's art.

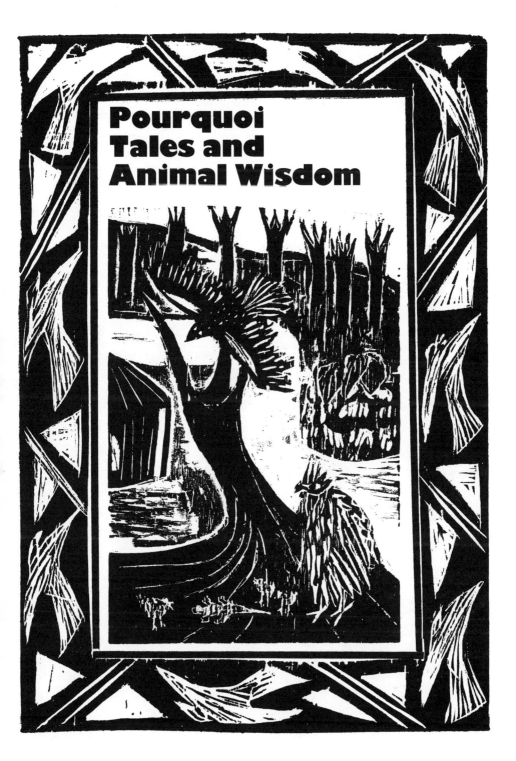

Pourquoi
Tales and
Animal Wisdom

How Chameleon Became a Teacher

Once upon a time, Crocodile and Chameleon were friends. Crocodile was very fond of sunbathing. Nothing gave him greater pleasure than to come splashing out of the water and to lie on the sand in bright sunshine. And whenever Crocodile came out of the water, Chameleon would come out of the bush and climb up a tree nearby. Soon, they would be heard chattering merrily and sending peals of laughter soaring through the air as though they had not a care in the world. Occasionally, they would be seen lying a short distance from each other, whispering, shaking their heads, or nodding as though the fate of the whole world hung upon the outcome of their consultations. Crocodile and Chameleon were very good friends.

One day, as they were about to go their separate ways, Crocodile invited Chameleon to dinner. "Come to my house, at the bottom of the lake," he said, "and my whole family will treat you to a delicious meal, and we'll have fun together afterwards. Jump right into the lake when you see me rise to the surface, and I will take you to my house." They agreed on a day and a time, Chameleon thanked Crocodile for his kindness, and they took leave of each other.

On the appointed day, Chameleon went to the shore of the lake, carrying a stick. While Chameleon waited, Crocodile gathered his wife and children together in their living room at the bottom of the lake and told them, "Rejoice! Rejoice! Chameleon, whom I have befriended, is coming to see us! He will be our special treat! I cannot tell you what a delicacy he will make! Chameleon meat is so tasty," he concluded, smacking his jaws and rolling his eyes.

So speaking, Crocodile went out to meet his friend. There was a great disturbance on the face of the lake as he came splashing into view close to the shore, his gigantic jaws wide apart. As though to test his friend, Chameleon threw his stick into the water. Believing that Chameleon himself had dived into the lake, Crocodile lunged forward and, with a blood-chilling crunch, closed his enormous jaws over the stick.

Trembling in terror, his heart racing furiously, Chameleon fled from the shore and scrambled up the closest tree. Then, taking cover and blending in with the foliage, he cried, "What would have become of me if I hadn't thrown my stick into the lake to test my friend! Thank God I didn't step in to meet Crocodile as he had instructed me, for I would have ended up in the bottom of his stomach instead of as a guest at his house. Take note! Take note, O world! Caution is the mother of safety!"

And so it was that Chameleon became a teacher of prudence and wisdom. Except when in danger, he treads ever so carefully, thinks long and hard before putting a foot forward, and takes on the local color wherever he happens to be.

In Fon folklore, *Chameleon is considered a representative of* Segbo Lissa, *creator of the world, the giver of wealth, and the* fountain of wisdom. In this pourquoi tale, the storyteller uses the wisdom of Chameleon to explain why it moves slowly and changes colors. But this tale is above all a cautionary tale that warns people against putting their trust in a "friend" without first submitting him or her to a test.

The Wrath Of the Hawk

Once upon a time, a baby hawk was taken ill. For days he lay shivering in the nest and would take neither food nor drink. Hawk, his mother, knew many plants, and never before had they failed her. With acacia leaves and other herbs and roots, she made various potions, but the little one went on shivering, getting weaker and thinner by the day. Like fire spreading through dry grass, the sickness consuming Baby Hawk seemed unquenchable.

It was then that Hawk decided to take the little one to Lizard, the greatest healer in the land. Lizard lived far, far away in a little village at the other end of the kingdom, but Hawk would go anywhere for the sake of her baby. Strapping him to her back with a piece of cloth, she took to her wings, singing as she flew,

> "I will fly all the way to the end of the earth,
> I will not rest until I have stilled your pain,
> And made you healthy and strong again!"

Hawk flew and flew, over rolling hills, fast-flowing streams, and towering forest-trees. She flew as she had never flown in her life, through whirlwinds and in sweltering heat, toward the dwelling of the greatest healer in the land.

Lizard was a little startled when Hawk came circling down over his compound, her baby strapped to her back. "To what do I owe this surprise visit?" Lizard asked, staring at the unexpected visitor.

"Baby Hawk is gravely ill," Hawk gasped. "Please help me!"

Lizard took the little bird and, holding him tight, listened to his heartbeat and his breathing. Nodding several times, he laid the little hawk on a sleeping-mat and sighed. "The little one is really ill," he said, "but it is not too late to save him."

Quickly Lizard called to his firstborn. "Run to the marketplace," he told him, "and buy a clay pot and seven cola nuts. Baby Hawk is gravely ill, and we must save him." Lizard's firstborn rushed out of the house as Lizard bustled about, gathering roots and leaves for a potion to cure Little Hawk's sickness.

Soon, Lizard had collected the roots and the leaves he needed. Only the clay pot and the cola nuts were missing. Lizard listened for his firstborn's footfalls, expecting him to come through the door any moment. And while he waited, Baby Hawk lay shivering on the sleeping-mat and would take neither food nor drink. To keep himself busy, Lizard checked the roots and the leaves he had gathered, to make sure none was missing. Then he listened again for the footfalls of his firstborn, but all he heard were Baby Hawk's labored breathing and Mother Hawk's despairing sobs. Putting his growing worry into words, he said,

"Why my firstborn isn't back I just don't know!
From here the market is a mere stone's throw!"

And so speaking, Lizard went out to look for his firstborn. He went straight to the marketplace and, rushing here and there, asked the potters and the cola-nut merchants, and everyone else if anyone had seen his firstborn. But no one had seen him. He looked in the surrounding bush and up and down countless paths, but his search was all in vain. As Lizard retraced his steps, he thought of the kidnappers and the prowling beasts known to prey on the unwary. A great fear came over him, and he cried:

> "Where, O where, is the little one gone?
> To him, I fear, mischief has been done!"

It was then that he saw in the distance Hen and a brood of chicks jabbing with their beaks at something on the ground. He came closer, and there, at the mercy of Hen and her ravenous chicks, lay the mangled body of his firstborn. Lizard uttered a heartrending cry. A great, seething rage seized hold of him, and he felt an impulse to fall upon Hen and her chicks and ring their necks, but he knew he was no match for them. He stood there awhile, at a loss for words, trembling all over, tears streaming down his face. Then he shouted,

> "You have dared to kill my beloved firstborn!
> By your cruelty are we to eternal enmity sworn!"

Hen and the chicks looked up a moment and then went on jabbing at their prey.

When Lizard returned home, he found Hawk, too, was weeping and tearing at her plumage, for Baby Hawk was no more. As Hawk listened to Lizard's tale of woe, her grief turned to a steaming rage against Hen and her chicks.

"In killing your firstborn, they killed my little one, too," Hawk cried. "May I die a thousand deaths if I do not give Hen a taste of the agony she has brought to you and me." No sooner had she uttered those words, than she unfurled her wings and took to the air, soaring higher and higher, until she vanished altogether.

A moment later, a speck was seen hovering high in the sky over the spot where Hen and her chicks stood pecking at the carcass of Lizard's firstborn. Then, like a bolt of lightening hurled out of the heavens, Hawk came swooping down to earth. There was an outburst of screeching and cheeping as Hen and her little ones scrambled for cover, and Hawk swept swiftly upward, clutching a chick in her claws. Hen struggled to fly after Hawk, but she was not made to fly. As she fell back to earth, cursing and screeching, Hawk's voice rang out, vindictive and triumphant,

"You have killed Lizard's little one and my own,
Now you must reap the pain you have sown.
At strife shall they be, my seed and your seed!
Death to all chicks: the price for your evil deed!"

And strife there has been between the descendants of Hawk and Hen ever since. Hardly a day goes by without a hawk swooping down to earth and snatching a chick away. And so it will be to the end of time, unless Hawk and Hen, both long gone out of this world, can find a way to achieve reconciliation in the Great Beyond.

This pourquoi tale *explains why hawks swoop down on chicks, a phenomenon familiar to people who live in rural areas. Like the fables of Aesop and La Fontaine or Native American tales, for example, Fon folktales often lend human characteris-*

tics to animals. Close interaction between human beings and animals, or between human beings and spirits, is an important characteristic of Fon folklore.

To the best of my knowledge, this is the only Fon tale where Lizard appears as a healer. Tortoise is the conventional healer and diviner, and he has been identified as such in "How Hare Drank Boiling Water and Married the Beautiful Princess."

How Hare Drank Boiling Water And Married The Beautiful Princess

My story takes flight over countries and kingdoms of long ago and alights on a princess. She was famous throughout her father's realm for her flashing eyes, her smooth, glowing complexion, her flowing, jet-black hair, and her soothing voice. All who saw her were captivated by her beauty, and many dreamed of having her for their wife. When the time came at last for her to be married, a great crowd gathered as men, beasts, and birds came to ask for her hand. They all vowed to make her the happiest woman in the world, and they all clamored around as each claimed to be the bravest, the strongest, and the most handsome. The king and the princess tried very hard to listen to everyone, but it was all very bewildering, and neither of them knew whom to choose.

So, in the end, the king decided he would have to set them a challenge. He thought long and hard, and then let it be known that whoever was brave enough to drink from a pot of boiling water was the one he would allow to marry his daughter. Messengers were sent out to spread the word far and wide throughout the kingdom, and eventually the day for the contest came. A clay pot was filled with water and put on a blazing wood fire right in the middle of the royal front yard. Then the princess and the king, dressed in their finest robes, were seated in the place of honor and waited.

It was not long before the water came to a boil, sending steam rising to the sky. Soon, a big crowd gathered around, and the herald proclaimed that all those who wished to try for the hand of the princess should come forward. A prince wearing beautiful clothes of fine silk stepped out of the crowd and walked boldly towards the fire. He was tall, strong, and good-looking. A hush fell on the crowd when, using a roll of cloth to cushion his hands, he seized the clay pot from the fire and lifted it straight to his lips. For a moment it looked as though he would succeed, but a blast of heat caught him in the face, and he quickly put the pot back on the fire again and walked away, his head bowed in shame. In turn, other princes, noblemen, warriors, and hunters came forward with great bravado, but sadly they all failed, one after another, and slunk away.

Then the king of the jungle, mighty Lion, broke out of the crowd, roaring at the top of his lungs, his mane glistening in the sun. He lifted the clay pot in his rough-padded paws and brought it closer and closer to his mouth, but the heat from the steam gushing out was more than even he could bear. Wincing and frowning, he, too, walked away as Eagle came circling down for his try. Eagle came as close as he could and pecked at the water, but the heat was such that he had to fly away, defeated.

There followed Leopard, Elephant, Monkey, Owl, Vulture, and many more princes, chiefs, and warriors, but none was brave enough.

As the fire burned down, more wood was added and more water was poured into the pot so that it was always filled to the brim with boiling water. There was great excitement when Tortoise emerged out of the crowd. Tortoise was known throughout the land as a great diviner, and rumor had it that he could make boiling water taste fresh and cool. Turning his head now to the left, now to the right, he made straight for the blazing fire, singing:

"The fire is burning and in the pot,
  The water is steaming, boiling hot.
  I go forth to take up the challenge,
  By the power of my venerable elders,
  The distinguished fellowship of diviners,
  May I carry the day, for a change!"

Rearing himself on his hind legs, tortoise lifted the pot and raised it to his mouth. But even he, with all his magical powers, was unequal to the ordeal.

The king couldn't go back on his proclamation, and as the day wore on it began to look as though the princess would have to do without a husband. It was then that Hare broke out of the crowd and went trotting up to the fire, his ears perked up, a mischievous smile flickering about his lips. He gave a little bow to the crowd and then turned and looked thoughtfully at the pot. The fire burned fiercely. The water boiled and bubbled, sending steam rising to the heavens. Hare took a roll of cloth to cushion his paws and then carefully lifted up the steaming pot, held it aloft, and started . . . talking.

First he turned to Lion and said,

"I have come to attempt what no one has done in living
    memory.
  I have come to drink boiling water and suffer death for my
    folly.

But for every act of folly there is a reason,
And mine is the power of love and passion.
I beg you, O King of the Jungle—upon my passing, tell my
   story,
Lest it fade from memory."

Lion agreed. In turn Hare asked Eagle, Tortoise, Monkey, Elephant, and all the other animals to tell his story, should he die after drinking the boiling water. All the animals quietly agreed, but that was not enough for Hare. He turned to the great princes, the warriors, and all the powerful people gathered there and begged them not to let his sacrifice sink into oblivion. He even spoke to the king and the princess, and each of them agreed.

Then, addressing the crowd as a whole, he concluded,

"Tell my story to your children
And your children's children,
Lest I die in vain.
For when we are gone,
Only our stories remain."

The crowd listened, enraptured by Hare's words, not realizing that the boiling water had slowly grown cold.

With the clay pot still held high, Hare bowed to the king, to the princess, and finally to the crowd. Then, he lowered the pot slowly to his lips and, with an expression of feigned agony, drank the water to the last drop. The crowd let out a great cheer as they rushed forward to acknowledge the hero. Hare had faced the terrible challenge and survived!

Hare was led to the palace with great majesty, and he and the beautiful princess were married. They lived happily together, and in time he became a great king, and they had many children, grandchildren, and great-grandchildren.

To this day, the people of that kingdom still haven't realized that during all the time Hare was imploring them to immortalize his brave deed in story, he was simply waiting for the water to cool!

This trickster tale *is a little unusual insofar as Hare, not Yogbo the Glutton, is the trickster. But Yogbo the Glutton himself could not have done better. This story dramatizes the power of storytelling.*

Here, as in many other Fon folktales, there is intermarriage between beasts and human beings. This is generally not so in Western European folktales, and it arguably points to a belief that beyond all the differences, there is a basic kinship between human beings and animals.

The Origin of Crocodiles, Fish, and Other Water Creatures

Once upon a time, in a village on the banks of a mighty river, a man sick unto death called his two sons together and told them:

"My end, O my children, is drawing near;
This is my command, please lend me an ear.
In all things, be true each to the other.
Loving kindness is the mark of a brother."

After the man died, the two brothers set up house together. Both were tillers of the soil, but the younger brother was rather frail of health and often afflicted with aches and pains, whereas the elder brother was strong and healthy. Although they were unequal in strength and one brought more out of the earth than the other, they lived in perfect harmony, sharing the fruits of their labor in equal measure. The spirit of the father, watching the children from the Great Beyond, must have smiled to see how faithfully they had complied with his command.

But then the elder brother felt lonely for a wife and married a beautiful maiden from a neighboring village. Right from the start, the woman took a dislike to her husband's brother, for she saw him as a burden. So she told her husband:

"You are strong, my beloved, hardworking and thrifty.
  That your brother is weaker is really a pity.
  Such a fool as you are, I have not seen anywhere.
  You have let your brother take more than his share."

To that, the elder brother replied:

"I am strong, my beloved, hardworking and thrifty.
  That my brother is weaker is surely a pity.
  But loving kindness is the mark of a brother.
  The bond of brotherhood nothing may sever."

Seeing that her words did not find favor with her husband, the woman held her peace, but deep in her heart hatred of her husband's brother grew and grew.

Another year went by, and the brothers remained close as ever. Ill-health confined the younger brother to his sleeping-mat for a great many days. Yet, he knew neither hunger nor want, for his elder brother took good care of him.

But the elder brother's wife would not have it so. After serving her husband food one evening, she told him:

"You are healthy, my beloved, hardworking and thrifty.
  That your brother cannot work as hard is a pity.
  But why, oh why, must you spoil and pamper him so?
  Let not one reap where another has labored to sow."

To that, the elder brother replied:

"I am healthy, my beloved, hardworking and thrifty.
  That my brother cannot work as hard is a pity.

But by the bond of brotherhood are we bound together.
In sickness and in health, let us be true each to the other.''

Again, seeing that her words did not find favor with her husband, the woman held her peace, but deep in her heart hatred of her husband's younger brother grew, and grew, and grew.

Another year went by, and the two brothers lived just as their father had commanded them, but poor health kept the younger out of work most of the time. The elder brother had to labor twice as hard as the year before, but he took good care of his brother and made sure he knew neither hunger nor want.

But the elder brother's wife would not have it so. One night, as they prepared to lie down and sleep, the woman told her husband:

> "The hour has come when you must make up your mind,
> Whether to keep your brother and the greatest fool remain,
> Or come with me, and become the wealthiest of your kind;
> But you cannot both your brother and your beloved
>   retain."

And to that, the elder brother made no answer. All night long, he tossed and turned on his sleeping-mat as love of his wife and loyalty to his younger brother fought for possession of his soul.

As a rooster's *cocorioko* came piercing the still pre-dawn air, the words of his wife echoed and re-echoed in his ears:

> "The hour has come when you must make up your mind,
> Whether to keep your brother and the greatest fool remain,
> Or come with me, and become the wealthiest of your kind;
> But you cannot both your brother and your beloved
>   retain."

And there came to him a vision of his beloved holding out to him sweet love in a new home and the promise of boundless riches. So taken was he with that vision that he shuddered to think of the long years of toil without rest and all the hardship he would have to endure should he, for the sake of his brother, let his beloved go.

And so it was that when his wife shook him awake and told him that she had packed all their provisions and their belongings, and that the canoe was ready, he closed his heart against his brother and followed her. The whole village was still sleeping when the elder brother and his wife set out on their long journey up the river.

The moon was shining bright, turning the surface of the river into a vast, silvery sheet rippling gently as the wind played over it. Not a soul was in sight, except for the two paddlers steering their canoe upstream toward a new home and a new life. But then the clouds, which at the outset were only a few splashes of pastel-blue scattered over the moonlit sky, grew larger and larger, taking on the dark hue of storm clouds. Soon, the radiant moon and the glittering stars dimmed to darkness, the wind gathered strength, and the river turned to a fearsome mass of surging water. The couple paddled fiercely, desperately, steering their way by the flashes of lightening crisscrossing the somber sky.

Neither spoke a word to the other, but the peril looming ahead made them both long for a return to the home they had deserted and the brother they had abandoned. They stayed their course, however, hoping to beat the odds by sheer force of will.

Suddenly, a deafening peal of thunder shook the heavens, and rain came hurtling down. The canoe quickly filled with water in spite of the travelers' frantic struggle to bail it out.

Seeing that their efforts bore no fruit, they threw their calabashes away and put on a final, frenzied burst of speed, hoping
against hope to race their way to safety. It was then that their
canoe, filled to the brim with water and tossed up and down by
the waves, sank slowly to the bottom of the river. Two voices
howling for help lingered in the air a moment and then were
heard no more.

Later that day, two scaly creatures with big snouts, globu-
lar eyes, and enormous tails swam out of the depths of the river
and crawled their way through the village to the house where
the elder brother and his wife had lived. Horror-stricken, the
villagers took up stones and sticks and chased the two crocodiles back to the river. The younger brother and all the villagers
with him wondered at the disappearance of his brother and his
wife and the appearance of the two monsters. But what the two
events had to do with each other remained a mystery to all.

Only after the village chief had sent for the *bokonon,* and
the oracle had been consulted, was the veil of mystery lifted.
This was what the diviner said:

> "A husband and wife crossing the river in a canoe angered
> the river-god by abandoning a close relative in his hour of
> need. Their canoe sank in stormy weather, and, drowning,
> the couple was turned into ugly, vicious water creatures,
> which to the end of time, would stand as reminders of their
> cruelty. But in his infinite kindness, the river-god changed
> the food and the provisions they were carrying into fish,
> crabs, and many other life-giving creatures to provide
> nourishment to the villagers, to all the people of the earth,
> and to the crocodiles, too, all year round."

And so it has been, to this day.

This story, like "The Dance of Poverty," dramatizes the importance of love and compassion and the perils of egotism and unkindness. The transformation of the elder brother and his wife into crocodiles on the one hand, and the transmutation of their provisions into sources of nourishment for all mankind and for crocodiles, too, is a powerful moral lesson charged with great irony. The story also illustrates the perception in traditional Fon society of the woman as a temptress. Traditional Fon society is a patriarchal society where women are usually blamed for many things. The story is often told, for example, of how a woman repeatedly bumped the sky with her pestle, causing it to rise to the position it occupies today.

Trickster Tales: Yogbo The Glutton

Why Goats Smell Bad

Long ago in the days of our ancestors, it was the custom to hold a feast of thanksgiving after all the crops had been gathered in. Each year, as the crops started to ripen, a sacrificial bull would be chosen from the king's herd of cattle and given to an honorable member of the community for safekeeping. Yogbo the Glutton would have given anything to be asked to keep the sacrificial bull, even for a day, but everyone knew that he was not to be trusted.

Yogbo was a smooth talker. He could talk a fierce dog into giving up a juicy bone, and he decided he was going to use his tongue to the full. Going from one household to another, Yogbo the Glutton would argue that he was no longer what he used to be and that no one could take better care of the sacrificial bull than he. Pleading to be given a chance to prove himself, he would conclude:

"I have changed in all but name,
  But you have stayed just the same.
  Long ago I was a byword for greed
  But today I take no more than I need."

Again and again, Yogbo the Glutton was laughed at and chased away, but he would not give up. Every unsuccessful plea, it seemed, sent honey-coated words rolling off his tongue and fastened the mask of sincerity ever more tightly on his face. Little by little, people started lending him an ear, and before long even the king was willing to give Yogbo the Glutton a chance.

So, when another year went by and the festival of thanksgiving drew near, a bull was taken from the king's herd and handed over to Yogbo for safekeeping. For a few days, Yogbo made a great show of tending to the bull, feeding him bundles of green, fresh-cut grass and washing him regularly to keep him clean. Those who had been a little doubtful of his intentions soon cast their suspicions to the wind, and everyone agreed that Yogbo was indeed the finest choice of caretaker ever made.

Even as people praised Yogbo the Glutton for taking such good care of the sacrificial bull, however, there came upon him a craving for roasted beef seasoned with salt, pepper, onion, and powdered shrimp.

"Well," he thought, sighing wearily and rubbing his stomach in a dreamy sort of way:

"Never put off until another day
Food that you can eat right away.
Too much praise is bad for the head
I will hold with my stomach instead."

Such were the thoughts that kept Yogbo rolling and turning on his sleeping-mat, three days before the festival of thanksgiving. Rising at first light, he took the sacrificial bull deep into the forest. And there, far from human eyes, he slaughtered it, roasted it, and ate it all by himself. Not a morsel did he spare, not even for his wife.

But no sooner had Yogbo eaten his fill, than a great fear came over him, for a voice came floating on the breeze, crying:

"You have eaten the sacrificial bull,
And now you must pay the price in full.
Beef may be more than praise is worth
But how will you escape the king's wrath?"

"How indeed will I escape the king's wrath?" Yogbo the Glutton repeated, his forehead creased with worry. For a long time he remained deep in thought, his chin cupped in the palm of his hand. Then, a mischievous smile lit up his face. He rose to his feet and went in search of an owl he had heard hooting in the distance. When Yogbo came upon him high in the treetop, he implored,

"I am a man in trouble,
Facing the wrath of the king of the land!
Sing a song, this time tomorrow,
To stay the executioner's hand,
And all the millet in my barn
I will cede to you and your kind!"

The owl would have nothing to do with Yogbo the Glutton, however; and muttering under his breath something about a wicked man caught in the toils of his own wickedness, the owl flew away, leaving Yogbo to face his troubles all by himself. It was then that a hawk came by, flying low over the treetops. Once again, Yogbo the Glutton raised his voice in supplication:

"I am a man in trouble,
Facing the wrath of the king of the land!
Sing a song, this time tomorrow,

To stay the executioner's hand,
And all the chicks on my farm
I will cede to you and your kind!"

But Yogbo was no luckier with the hawk than he had been with the owl, and yet, he would not give up. Plunging farther into the forest, he came upon a canary singing merrily in a bush. Once again, Yogbo the Glutton pleaded for help:

"I am a man in trouble,
Facing the full force of the law of the land!
Sing a song, this time tomorrow,
To stay the executioner's hand,
And all the grains in my barn
I will offer you and your kind!"

The canary stopped singing, and Yogbo went closer, begging and pleading for the songster's help.

They spoke in hushed tones for a long time. And when Yogbo the Glutton finally took leave of the songbird, he went back home, not like a criminal in fear of his life, but with a light step, like a warrior bearing tidings of victory.

The news of what Yogbo had done to the sacrificial bull traveled before him, and members of the royal guard seized hold of him the moment he got back to the village. Meeting in an extraordinary session later that evening, the king's council sentenced Yogbo to death. The next day, in spite of his wife's supplications, Yogbo was led, shackled and blindfolded, to the foot of the old baobab tree where rites and executions were performed. Men, women, and children had gathered to witness the punishment of the man who had pulled the wool over the eyes of the king and all his subjects and eaten all by himself a bull big enough to feed the whole community.

Soon, the king and the members of his council sat in the place of honor. A hush fell on the crowd as the royal executioner, holding his sword aloft, strode towards the baobab tree to await the order that would seal Yogbo's fate. No sooner had he taken up position than a canary flying overhead alighted swiftly on the baobab tree and burst into song:

"Shed not a drop of this man's blood,
　Nor touch a single hair on his head.
　For whoever shall give the order,
　Together with the executioner,
　Nay—witnesses far and near alike
　Shall face a most terrible plight:
　Death and disease—a fearsome price."

The executioner broke out in cold sweat, and his eyes grew large. A shadow passed over the face of the king, and shivers ran down his spine. And while the crowd stood spellbound with amazement, he announced, after a hasty consultation with his advisers, that he had decided to set Yogbo the Glutton free.

Later that evening, Yogbo invited to a feast in his house the canary who had saved him from the executioner's keen-edged sword. He fed him rice and millet, and, as there was a chill in the air, invited him to warm himself by the fireside. But while Yogbo the Glutton entertained the songbird with rude remarks about the king, the executioner, and those who had come to watch his execution, he suddenly felt hungry for a well-roasted bird. He stared greedily at his unsuspecting guest. Then, muttering under his breath that it was foolish to postpone to another day food that he could eat right away, he seized the canary and threw him into the fire.

That night, as Yogbo the Glutton lay on his sleeping-mat,

he was seized with a terrible stomachache. To his horror, he watched his stomach swell and swell until it hit the roof! The *Bokonon* was immediately sent for, and, after consulting the oracle, he requested a gourd and a needle. While Yogbo lay groaning and writhing in agony, the medicine man pierced his distended belly with the needle. A foul-smelling gas came whistling its way out, and the *Bokonon* swiftly put the mouth of the gourd over the wound to collect it. After all the gas had gone into the gourd and the medicine man had sealed it, a flock of canaries flew out of Yogbo's stomach, amid the whir of a thousand wings. As they came out, each bird jabbed at the glutton's belly with its beak, causing him to scream and beg for mercy.

After the last canary had flown out and Yogbo's stomach had sunk down to a manageable size, the *Bokonon* thrust the sealed gourd into Yogbo's hands, saying, "Take this to the shore of the river and break it over the head of any creature you can find. A terrible curse has been laid upon you. Only by doing as I have told you will that curse be undone."

Early in the morning, Yogbo the Glutton went forth to the bank of the river, cradling the gourd of foul-smelling gas in his hands as though it were the most precious jewel ever to have graced an emperor's crown. Soon, Hare came out of the bush to slake his thirst. Yogbo came singing and dancing up to him, and smiling from ear to ear, invited Hare to join in the dance of victory. But Hare suspected there was wickedness in the wind and turned the invitation down. Then Lion came by and Yogbo invited him to dance, but Lion was not for dancing. There followed Monkey, Deer, Buffalo, Hyena, Snake, Vulture, and a great many other birds and animals, but they all suspected a trap and refused to dance.

As the day wore on, Yogbo grew increasingly desperate,

for it looked as though no creature on the face of the earth was going to fall for his trick and relieve him of his curse. But then Goat came down the path. Yogbo came singing and dancing up to him, praising him and begging him to join in the dance of victory.

Now, Goat was a gifted dancer, and the sound of music always made his spine tingle. "What victory?" Goat asked, a little surprised to see Yogbo the Glutton singing and dancing all by himself at the edge of the river. By way of an answer, Yogbo sang all the more sweetly and danced with great relish, waving his gourd as though it were a priceless trophy. Goat could contain himself no longer, and soon he was dancing as he had never danced before, rearing himself on his hind legs and turning round and round, his eyes half-closed, a self-satisfied smile playing at the corners of his mouth.

Singing at the top of his lungs and cheering him on, Yogbo raised the gourd high in the air and, with all his might, broke it over Goat's head. As Yogbo the Glutton took to his heels, Goat felt himself enveloped by an overpowering stench. Gasping and spluttering, he jumped into the river and washed himself vigorously, but the smell held fast. Goat plunged deeper into the river and rubbed against the rocks, but the foul smell still clung to him. He rushed out of the water and rolled in the grass and sand of the riverbank till he grew tired and cranky. When Goat at last got up, some of the bad smell had come off, but most of it remained.

That is why, to this day, goats give off a very bad smell.

This pourquoi tale *shows Yogbo the Glutton at his worst: repaying good deeds with savage ingratitude and preying on the* *unwary—but that is in the nature of tricksters. The tale jumps from the bull to the king's wrath to the canary and to the goat. Fon folktales, unlike their Western counterparts, sometimes have a tendency to ramble on, but that in no way obscures the storyteller's point. What happened to Goat is very interesting in that respect. He would not have fallen victim to Yogbo's wiles if he had exercised more self-control and had not danced with his eyes half-closed or with such abandon.*

Graceful, elegant dancing is held in high regard among the Fon, and many of their folktales involve song and dance. It is interesting that Goat's dance in "Why Goats Smell Bad" and Atchanminanguey's dance in "The Dance of Poverty" both have negative outcomes. Goat is punished for his foolishness and his vanity, and Atchanminanguey fails to get his wealth and his crown back from the spirit because he is ungrateful and unkind.

The Name-Guessing Contest

My story takes flight over countries and kingdoms of long ago and alights on four princesses, quadruplets with big, sparkling eyes, radiant, coppery complexions, and stately bearings. They were like no other princesses on the face of the earth, for no one knew their names, not even their mother or the king, their father. When they were born, they were named according to tradition, but as soon as they could talk, they told their parents:

"The names you gave us at birth are alien to us,
And we shall not answer to them.
Before we were born, we had been given names
In the Great Beyond,
But those names will have to remain a secret to all.
You would do anything to know what we are called,
But no power on earth can make us reveal our names."

Their parents knew that what they had said was no idle talk, but it was something they found difficult to live with. Every man, every woman, and everything under the sun answered to a given name, but their quadruplets would answer to none! How would they introduce them to the multitude who came to the palace every day? What would they say when someone asked, "What is your daughter's name?" Would they say "I don't know?" Who had ever heard of a man being unable to tell the name of a child that was flesh of his flesh and bone of his bone? It was all very awkward, but what could they do?

The royal parents tried eavesdropping, but it was to no avail. They instructed servants to spy on the girls, but that, too, yielded nothing. They even paid various maidens to befriend them in order to wheedle their names out of them, but these efforts were all in vain. And the older the four princesses grew, the more keenly the king felt the embarrassment of not knowing his daughters' names.

As they came of age, all the men in the kingdom longed to take one or the other to wife, for they were very beautiful, but the king could not bear to part with his daughters without knowing their names. One night, as he lay in bed wracking his mind for a solution to the mystery surrounding his daughters' names, an idea occurred to him. He thought about it for a moment, frowning in concentration. Then a smile broke over his face. That night, he slept soundly for the first time in many years.

The next day, a royal proclamation went forth to the four corners of the kingdom: The time had come for the king's four daughters to get married. Immediately following the festival of thanksgiving, a seven-day name-guessing contest would be held. Whoever could guess the names of the king's four daughters would marry them. No bride price would be required.

On the appointed day, a big crowd gathered on the royal grounds. In the center, four stools had been arranged in a semicircle for the four princesses. In front of the seats was a jar filled to the brim with palm wine, and next to the jar, a calabash was laid on a mat.

Soon, the king, the mother, and the members of the king's council came out of the palace in stately procession and took their seats in the place of honor. Then, the four princesses were led to their stools, and the king's spokesman explained the rules of the contest. Each contender had to step up to the jar, scoop up palm wine with the calabash, and, calling out each princess's name, offer her a sip. Each princess would get up and take a sip from the calabash when called by her real name.

A deathly silence prevailed when a prince from a neighboring kingdom first stepped forward and, scooping up palm wine from the first jar, called out, "Dossa! This is for you. Come and take a sip!"

No princess, got up, however, and the prince retraced his steps, defeated. There followed a great many contenders— warriors, chiefs, hunters, farmers, blacksmiths, goldsmiths, merchants, and many others. But all the fancy names by which they addressed the princesses fell on deaf ears. Three days went by, and no one had managed to guess the names of the four princesses. It was then that Yogbo the Glutton decided to take action.

That day, Yogbo's best friend, Yai, had jokingly promised him enough food to fill his bottomless pit of a stomach as a reward for help in uncovering the names of the princesses. Now Yogbo was known never to forgo a chance for a good meal, so he took Yai at his word.

It was common knowledge that the four princesses were in the habit of going down to the river every morning at the first light of dawn to fetch water, and Yogbo decided to turn that to good account. The next day, as the four princesses set out for the river, Yogbo shadowed them. Soon, they reached a mango tree laden with mangoes. The four sisters scrambled for the ripe fruits lying on the ground and ate them with great relish. By the time they had resumed their journey, Yogbo had conceived a scheme to solve the mystery of their names.

On the fifth day of the name-guessing contest, Yogbo woke up early and hurried to the mango tree, carrying a huge bag. He wanted to make a clean sweep of the ripe fruits on the ground and on the tree, but not a single mango did he find. The four princesses had taken everything.

On the sixth day of the contest, Yogbo woke up before the first cockcrow and rushed to the mango tree. He had better luck that day, for the ground was strewn with ripe mangoes. He quickly collected them and stuffed them into his bag. Then, he scrambled up the tree, picked all the ripening mangoes, and shoved them, too, into his bag. Finally, he climbed to the top of the tree and hid among the foliage.

Soon, the four princesses came down the path, arguing good-humoredly over who was going to get the most mangoes.

"Today, I am going to get more mangoes than all of you," one said.

"No, I am going to get so many mangoes you will swoon with envy," said another.

"None of you can compete with me when it comes to picking fruits off a tree. You all know that," the third princess said.

"You all like to talk, don't you?" the fourth princess said. "Wait and see how I am going to put you all to shame."

When they got to the mango tree, however, not a mango was to be found.

"Someone must have come here in the middle of the night

and carried off all the mangoes," they cried. "If only we can catch the wretched thief, we will give him such a tongue-lashing that he will never touch a mango again!"

It was then that Yogbo reached into his enormous bag, seized a mango, and, taking aim, let it fall close to one of the princesses. She grabbed it with both hands before the others could make a dash for it.

"Avodahossihoue has got a mango!" they cried.

A broad smile lit up Yogbo's face as he made a mental note of the name and quickly grabbed another mango, took aim again, and let it fall. A second princess went down on her knees and seized it.

"Vovohoungbenan has got one, too!" her sisters cried.

Yogbo also memorized that name and quickly dropped another fruit.

"Noumedonkpevi has got a mango in her turn!" her sisters cried. Yogbo committed that name, too, to memory, and let a fourth mango fall.

"Now Minklinmandi has got a mango, too," her sisters exclaimed.

The four princesses lingered awhile under the tree, but no more mangoes fell. And while they searched the branches, Yogbo silently went over the four names, grinning from ear to ear:

"Vovohoungbenan,
Minklinmandi,
Avodahossihoue,
Noumedonkpevi."

When at last the princesses went on their way, Yogbo stole down the tree and quickly vanished into the bush. Soon, he was standing on his best friend's doorstep, trembling with excitement.

"I have a marvelous gift for you if you will keep your word," Yogbo whispered breathlessly into Yai's ear. "I will tell you the names of the four princesses if you will prepare forty-one delicious meals for me. Now hurry unless you want me to take my gift to someone else."

Yai gripped Yogbo's hands as though he were afraid he might melt into thin air. His heart beat wildly, and his head swarmed with visions of the whole land celebrating his marriage to the four princesses. But then he felt a sharp pain of doubt, and, searching Yogbo's face, he said:

"I will kill you if it's a joke you have come to play on me, for this is no joking matter!"

"Give me plenty of food, you fool, and the four princesses will be yours!" Yogbo replied.

Quickly, Yai whispered instructions to his mother and sisters and soon, forty-one steaming dishes were laid out on a mat for Yogbo the Glutton.

When he had eaten all the food and washed it down with countless calabashes of palm wine, Yogbo beckoned to his friend and told him the names of the four princesses.

"One princess goes by the name of Vovohoungbenan; the second one is called Minklinmandi; the third, Avodahossihoue; and the fourth, Noumindonkpevi. These are the names you must call out when the moment comes."

As soon as Yogbo left, Yai made a song in order to fix the four names in his mind. And the next day, as he set out for the king's palace, he sang quietly to himself:

"What Yogbo the trickster has told me,
The names he heard on a mango tree,

Yogbo the trickster, the riddle solver,
They have entered my ears.

One princess is named Vovohoungbenan,
Another goes by the name Minklinmandi,
The third one is called Avodahossihoue,
And the fourth is named Noumindonkpevi

These are the names he has told me,
The names he heard on a mango tree,
Yogbo the trickster, the riddle solver.
And they have entered my ears."

When Yai reached the arena, it was packed with people. The name-guessing contest had entered its final day, and a large crowd had gathered to see whether any of the few remaining contestants was going to succeed where so many had failed.

Soon, it was his turn. In a few determined strides, Yai walked up to the jar of palm wine. Then, he seized the calabash, scooped up some of the palm wine and, fixing the four princesses with his gaze, called out:

"Vovohoungbenan! Come and take a sip!"

One of the princesses rose to her feet and walked slowly toward Yogbo's friend, her mouth agape. A murmur of disbelief spread through the crowd as Yai called out in quick succession:

"Minklinmandi! Come and take a sip!"

"Avodahossihoue! Come and take a sip!"

"Noumindonkpevi! Come and take a sip!"

For a moment, the crowd stood still, as though petrified. But when the king beckoned to Yai in recognition of his victory, the crowd surged forward, rending the air with exclamations of wonder and envy.

Yai and the four princesses were married in a sumptuous

wedding ceremony shortly thereafter. In time he became king, and he and his four wives had many children and lived in harmony into old age. But hardly a day went by without the four sisters asking him: "How did you manage to get our names?"

And Yai would smile to himself and say solemnly:

"With a loving heart and a strong will,
 You can grasp all truths
 And solve all mysteries,
 Just as the earth knows why
 Mangoes fall from mango trees."

This is the only Fon folktale *I know of where Yogbo the Glutton does a good deed, albeit a self-interested one. This tale tells us that Yogbo, the archetypal villain in Fon folklore, is not entirely without his good features. With regard to the four princesses, the story reminds us that twins, triplets, quadruplets, and others of multiple birth are no ordinary human beings. They are venerated as minor gods in the Fon pantheon. That is why the quadruplets' claim to have been named in the Great Beyond is taken seriously in the story. The story also dramatizes the importance of names among the Fon. In Fon culture, there is a belief that anyone who knows your real name has power over you. That is why the Fon don't tell strangers or evil-minded people their real names.*

The ending of the story, which leaves the princesses guessing how their husband managed to get their names, is my contribution. The original tale ends with Yai marrying the four princesses after he won the name-guessing contest. As a story-

teller, I decided the story would be more interesting if I brought out the crucial question on the minds of the four sisters and had their husband answer it with a witty statement that would turn the tables on them.

How Yogbo The Glutton Was Tricked

Once upon a time, there lived a girl named Alougba. She was a hardworking little girl with keen bright eyes—a delight to her parents and relatives. No chore was too difficult for her, nor was she known to rest until her task was done. Alougba's favorite chore was to go to the forest to fetch firewood in the company of other girls from neighboring villages.

One day, she foolishly gathered too much firewood so that she couldn't keep up with the others and was left behind. A veil of darkness was descending upon the countryside, and in the tall, ghost-like trees, witch birds pierced the air with their cries. The load Alougba was carrying was heavy, the distance long, and there was not a soul in sight. But Alougba wasn't going to give up. On she trudged through the gathering dusk with the load on her head, her neck pressed back into her shoulders, her body drenched in sweat.

To keep up her spirits, she sang to herself. Soon, her throat was dry, and she felt an increasingly desperate craving for a few swallows of cool water. Looking around, she caught sight of a massive baobab tree with a yawning hole in its trunk. "I hope there is water in the hole," Alougba thought, "for I am dying of thirst."

Throwing her burden to the ground, she rushed toward the tree, and to her joy and great relief found the hole filled almost to the brim with sparkling water. Alougba reached out and plunged her right hand into the hole to scoop up some of the cool, soothing water, but when she tried to withdraw her hand, behold! it got stuck. She plunged her left hand into the hole to free her right hand, but it, too, got stuck. Helpless and handless, Alougba broke into tears, and her cries floated away on the still evening air.

It was then that Yogbo, a trickster well-known for gluttony, came from behind a clump of trees, grinning broadly at the success of his trap. He gestured for Alougba to calm down. "Oh, what's the matter now, little girl?" he said in his oily voice.

"Please help me," Alougba sobbed. "I was going to scoop up some water to drink, and now both my hands are stuck."

"You have got your hands into some sort of glue, I see . . . I wonder where the glue came from," he laughed, rubbing his hands with half-concealed glee, his eyes shining with cunning.

Mumbling a few magic words, Yogbo pulled Alougba's hands free, but instead of letting her go, he brought a drum from behind the tree and stuffed her inside. And, for many days, while Alougba's parents and relatives and all the people in the village were looking for the missing girl, Yogbo went from one village to another, beating his drum.

Whenever Yogbo reached a compound, he would beat his drum until people gathered around him, and he would ask, his voice breaking with excitement, "Do you want to hear a drum that sings like a human being?"

And the people would say, "A drum that sings like a human being! Yes . . . Let's hear it!"

"Bring a lot of food and a lot of palm wine!" Yogbo the Glutton would reply, "for you cannot hear my singing drum unless you pay for it!"

Once his demand was satisfied, Yogbo would set the drum on the ground in front of him and beat it for a brief moment, commanding: "Drum, my singing drum, sing a song." And the drum would break into song:

> "Adjai, my father, Seyi, my mother,
> I am inside Yogbo's drum.
> I sing at Yogbo's command,
> I am the one this song is coming from.
> Daybreak will not come,
> And yet the sun has risen.
> Nightfall hangs back,
> But the moon is on the horizon.
> I sing at Yogbo's command,
> I am the singer in the drum.
> It is your missing daughter
> This song is coming from."

If Yogbo had a single grain of common sense, he would never have let his captive sing that song, for she was singing for help. But Yogbo had no common sense except for the counsel of his bottomless stomach.

Before Alougba's disappearance became common knowledge, people marveled at Yogbo's singing drum, and children followed him everywhere, for Alougba's words had not sunk in. And wherever he went, he was given money and plenty of food, for that was what he demanded in payment for making his

drum sing. And Yogbo would not touch his drum until he had
received his due.

As word of Alougba's disappearence spread, however, people exchanged knowing looks as they listened to the plaintive
wail of the drum.

One day, without being aware of it, Yogbo reached Alougba's village. Alougba's parents had prepared with great fore-
thought. Cunningly, they extended a warm welcome to the
trickster and cooked delicious dishes for him: roast beef seasoned with pepper, onion, garlic, and powdered shrimp;
pounded cassava served with goatmeat sauce, and many other
choice dishes. They also provided plenty of palm wine. Yogbo
licked his lips as his hosts laid out the food before him.

As they had expected, Yogbo ate ravenously, gluttonously.
He ate as though starved since the day he was born. With loud
smacking sounds, he hurled huge chunks of meat and plateful
upon plateful of food down to the pit of his voluminous stomach. He ate and drank until his stomach ached. Then he belched
and fell asleep.

The moment Alougba's parents had been waiting for had
come. While Yogbo was snoring and dreaming of mountains of
food and torrents of palm wine, Adjai, Alougba's father, slit
open Yogbo's drum and delivered his beloved daughter. Then
he filled the drum with stones and patched it up. Seyi, rejoicing
at the recovery of her child, bathed Alougba and massaged her
with a scented, soothing ointment. She then gave her food and
water and hid her in the bedroom.

When Yogbo finally woke up, he took his drum and went
on his way. He reached the next village and again demanded
food and palm wine as the price for entertaining people with his
singing drum, and his demand was satisfied. But when he laid

his hands on the drum, commanding, "Drum, my singing drum, sing a song," there was a stony silence. Yogbo shook the drum with desperate determination, for he knew he would have to say goodbye to the pleasures of gluttony unless he could make his drum sing. "Drum, my singing drum, sing a song," Yogbo commanded hoarsely.

But what he got in answer was not a song, but the harsh sound of stones clashing with stones.

With the angry, jeering crowd at his heels, Yogbo fled in shame back to Alougba's village. Standing outside her parents' hut, he loudly berated them and accused them of foul play.

Adjai and Seyi, looking at first innocent and then angry, denied having done anything to his singing drum. And so it was that Yogbo the Glutton, a man of unsurpassed greed and cunning, finally met his match and had to hold his peace.

This tale shows how *Yogbo can be defeated: by superior cunning. It is interesting that Alougba's parents use food as a bait for the trickster. Food is a very important part of life among the Fon. And in giving Yogbo plenty of food and drink, they hit Yogbo at his most vulnerable spot. It is one of the conventions of Fon folklore that Yogbo is immune to violence. And whenever Yogbo is threatened with violence, he is saved at the eleventh hour, as he is for example in "Why Goats Smell Bad."*

How Yogbo The Glutton Met His Death

My story takes flight, over countries and kingdoms of long ago and alights on Yogbo the Glutton walking through the forest in search of food. The meager provisions in his barn had long been exhausted, and no one was willing to help him out. He had gone to the village chief and begged him for food, but the chief said he had no food to lend a wicked man. He had gone to all the peasants in the village and to anyone who had food to spare, but wherever he went, people shut the door in his face. It was a common saying in the village that

"Lion and leopard would bid farewell to raw meat
Before Yogbo would cease from cunning and greed."

Again and again, Yogbo the Glutton had proclaimed that he had washed himself clean of cunning and wickedness:

"My wickedness and my greed—those are things of the past!
Today Yogbo is a man true as gold, worthy of trust, at last!"

Yet, no one believed him. In sheer desperation Yogbo had promised to return at the next harvest ten times the quantity of grains anyone would be kind enough to lend him. But his words brought nothing but scornful laughter. So he decided to try his luck in the forest.

The sun had barely raised himself above the horizon when Yogbo set out, and now daylight was on the wane, but Yogbo the Glutton had found nothing to eat. His face was hollow, worn with care, and his voluminous stomach was wrinkled all over like a shrunken pouch. The squirrels, the field rats, and other animals had gone nowhere near the traps he had set for them. No bird had flown within striking distance of his sling-shot, and all wild fruits seemed to have hidden themselves away. Could it be that the guardian spirit of the forest had decided to lend a helping hand to the people trying to starve him to death? Yogbo wondered.

Yogbo's heart pounded wildly at the thought, and his forehead shimmered with beads of cold sweat as a vision came to him: The guardian spirit of the forest was barring his way to a feast to which everyone else had been invited.

"If you kill me now, you will lose your reputation for fair-mindedness," he whimpered in supplication to the spirit.

> "My wickedness and my greed—those are things of the
> past!
> Today Yogbo is a man true as gold, worthy of trust at
> last!"

Yogbo repeated his supplication again and again as he wandered here and there, looking for food.

Suddenly, in a clearing in the forest, he stumbled upon a gigantic mushroom gleaming black in the paling radiance of daylight. It was *houto*, a delicacy traditionally reserved for special occasions. Yogbo stopped dead in his tracks, his mouth wide open, his head swimming with visions of dishes piled high with chunks of delicious *houto*.

The sheer size of the mushroom and its very color should have given Yogbo the Glutton pause, for it was no ordinary mushroom. The story was often told of a gigantic, unusually black *houto* that sometimes appeared to gluttons to tempt them to their doom. To call it by name within hearing distance was to sentence oneself to death. If Yogbo were a little careful, he would be in no danger, but Yogbo was ruled by his stomach, not his head. Leaping toward the mushroom with arms outstretched, he exclaimed:

"Fancy chancing upon you in my hour of need!
  O! wondrous *houto,* you're a godsend indeed!"

But no sooner had Yogbo the Glutton called the mushroom by name than he dropped to the ground, lifeless! As he lay there in the dust, the mushroom took pity on him, however, and brought him back to life. Then, calling him by his name, it said:

"You know not what you have just done!
  You are the biggest fool under the sun!
  Let this be a lesson to you, day and night!
  Whoever I hear call my name loses his life!"

Yogbo was glued to the ground with fright. In silent prayer he begged the earth to open up and hide him in her bowels, but his prayer went unanswered. Fearing the spirit-mushroom might have a change of mind and thrust him back into the world of the dead, Yogbo the Glutton tottered to his feet. Walking backward to increase the distance between himself and the spirit-mushroom, he said in a trembling voice:

"Thank you, most merciful spirit, for sparing my life!
   Your name I will hold sacred, by day and by night!"

When Yogbo the Glutton had gone far enough, he turned and took to his heels. Soon he was out of breath and sat under a tree to ponder his hair-raising experience. The words of the mushroom-spirit echoed and re-echoed in his ears:

"Let this be a lesson to you day and night!
   Whoever I hear call my name loses his life!"

"I could have died on an empty stomach!" Yogbo cried with a shudder. "It is a thousand times better to look for food on an empty stomach than to die on an empty stomach!"

   It was then that Yogbo caught sight of a buffalo in the distance. He peered hungrily at the beast for a moment, frowning in concentration. Then he sprang to his feet and went hurrying toward the buffalo, his eyes gleaming with mischief.

   When Yogbo the Glutton got close enough, he challenged the buffalo to a wrestling match, saying, "I know you are one of the strongest animals in the forest, but I tell you I will throw you to the ground with my little finger."

   Now the buffalo was a feisty fellow, always spoiling for a fight. "What has put that silly idea into your head?" he sneered, eyeing the skinny Yogbo with amazement. "Come on, then," the buffalo snorted, squaring up to his challenger.

   "Hold on," Yogbo said smiling. "Hear me out."

"Over there beyond that clump of giant trees,
   There is wrestling space and a gentle breeze.
   When we get there, I'll raise a finger in the air,
   And you must shout '*Houto!*' loud and clear.

Only then will our wrestling get under way
That's the rule, simple, clear as the light of day."

Buffalo found Yogbo's rule very strange, but he followed Yogbo
to the arena he had indicated, a few steps from the spot where
the spirit-mushroom stood. Yogbo the Glutton raised his finger,
and the buffalo, squaring up to him, bellowed 'Houto!' the
death-dealing name. That was the last bellow he ever gave.
Beaming with joy, Yogbo the Glutton dragged the dead buffalo
away, roasted it, and ate it all by himself.

For many days thereafter Yogbo was well supplied with
meat. In quick succession he challenged a leopard, a boa, a lion,
an elephant, and many other animals to wrestling matches and
sent them to their deaths, one after another. Soon, the forest
was buzzing with rumors of a fearsome hunter bent on hunting
the forest animals to extinction. A meeting was held, and word
went forth, warning all animals to be on their guard against
hunters. As a result, many a hunter returned from the hunt
empty-handed again and again. But Yogbo never lacked for
meat, for his weapon was not the common bow and arrow, but
trickery.

One day, however, a monkey who had been spying on
Yogbo the Glutton discovered his secret. Hidden in a tree, he
saw Yogbo play his deadly trick on a boar and decided to give
the glutton a taste of his own trickery. The day had been singu-
larly unfruitful, except for the boar. The moment Yogbo saw
the monkey swinging from a tree, his mouth watered, and his
stomach called for well-roasted monkey meat.

"I know you are a great wrestler, but I tell you I will throw
you to the ground with nothing but my little finger," he called
out to the monkey, pushing out his chest and beating it boast-
fully.

"You are nothing but a dead leaf challenging the wind to a fight, and I will show you what I mean right now," the monkey replied, jumping down from the tree and squaring up to Yogbo.

"Hold it," Yogbo said, smiling cunningly at the success of his ploy:

"Over there, beyond that clump of giant trees.
There is wrestling space and a gentle breeze.
When we get there, I'll raise a finger in the air.
And you must shout '*Houto!*' loud and clear.
Only then will the wrestling get under way.
That's the rule, simple, clear as the light of day."

The monkey followed Yogbo, but when they reached the appointed place and Yogbo raised his finger in the air, the monkey remained silent. Yogbo could not understand. "Remember the rule," Yogbo scolded, raising his finger in the air a second time.

"But I have forgotten," the monkey stammered, pretending to wrack his brain for the word he was supposed to call out. "No," said he, shaking his head, "I cannot remember."

Yogbo grabbed the monkey's hand and, dragging him out of earshot of the spirit-mushroom, told him:

"When I raise my little finger in the air,
You must shout '*Houto!*' very loud and clear.
Only then will the wrestling get under way.
That's the rule, simple, clear as the light of day."

But when they returned to the wrestling arena and Yogbo raised his finger in the air, the monkey once again said nothing. Yogbo was angry. "What is the matter now!" he shouted at the monkey, barely controlling himself. "Don't tell me you have forgotten what I have just repeated to you!"

"I am very sorry," the monkey said, holding his head in his hands in feigned concentration. "For the life of me, I cannot recall what it is I am supposed to say. It has gone clean out of my head."

"What a fool," Yogbo the Glutton muttered under his breath, as he dragged the monkey away to repeat to him once again the word he must shout for the wrestling to begin:

"When I raise my little finger in the air,
You must shout '*Houto!*' loud and clear.
Only then will the wrestling get under way.
That's the rule, simple, clear. Now do as I say!"

But when they went back and Yogbo raised his little finger in the air, there was dead silence. Then the monkey threw up his hands in feigned despair and whimpered, "I do not know what is the matter with me today. . . . I have become very forgetful, all of a sudden."

Yogbo the Glutton was beside himself with anger. "What a fool!" he shouted, stamping his feet. "What on earth makes it so hard for you to say '*Houto!*'"

"Ahhhhhhhhhhh!" he cried as soon as he spoke the death-dealing word. "I have killed myself!" Yogbo waved his hands frantically in an attempt to catch the word and swallow it, but it was all in vain. A word is like an egg. Once you let it fall to the ground, it cannot be gathered back into its shell. As Yogbo fell lifeless to the ground, the monkey went leaping and bounding to tell the other animals the tale of Yogbo's death and how it had come to pass.

This is the only Fon story *where Yogbo, the archetypal trickster of Fon folklore, dies, for Yogbo is considered immortal. Nothing except cunning can get the better of him. Perhaps the main reason why he cannot be killed is that he is a witty, resourceful character with an irrepressible zest for life. It is important that he should live, for in spite of his shortcomings, this character is the essence of life. If he dies, the storyteller's repertoire will be very poor indeed. Yet, since the Fon also hold to the belief that nothing lasts forever, even Yogbo himself must die. It is interesting that it is a monkey who gets the better of Yogbo. In Fon folklore, monkeys are said to be very clever, second only to Man. The story is often told of how God had intended to put Monkey in the place of Man, but changed his mind because Monkey was too boastful.*